HOW TO WRITE A RESUME IF YOU DIDN'T GO TO COLLEGE

HOW TO WRITE
A RESUME IF YOU DIDN'T
GO TO COLLEGE

Richard H. Beatty

WILEY

John Wiley & Sons, Inc.

Published by John Wiley & Sons, Inc., Hoboken, New Jersey.
Published simultaneously in Canada.

Library of Congress Cataloging-in-Publication Data:

Beatty, Richard H., 1939–
    How to write a resume if you didn't go to college / Richard H. Beatty.
      p. cm.
    Includes index.
    ISBN 0-471-44607-6 (pbk.)
    1. Resumes (Employment).   I. Title.
    HF5383.B3244   2003
    650.14′2—dc21

                                              2003049674

Printed in the United States of America.

10 9 8 7 6 5 4 3 2 1

To the Hourly-Paid Worker,
the Heart and Soul
of the American Workforce

Preface

It amazes me that there are literally hundreds of resume books on the market today that focus exclusively on teaching professionals and managers how to write a resume, but hardly any that offer assistance to hourly paid workers. This book is the exception!

The irony is that hourly paid employees (both blue and white collar) comprise over 75 percent of the U.S. workforce. They are truly the heart, soul, and backbone of the American economy, and yet, job search books have largely tended to ignore their needs. This book, however, reverses this trend, by focusing exclusively on the resume-writing needs of this special group.

In Chapter 1, you learn why it is now becoming extremely important for all hourly paid workers, both white collar and blue collar, to have a resume. The rapid shift of traditional newspaper job ads to the Internet, which employers are finding both considerably cheaper and more effective than newspaper advertising, is now requiring even blue-collar workers to have an effective resume document. Additionally, the tight labor market and increasingly intense competition greatly favors those workers having a strong resume that effectively markets their skills and capabilities.

When it comes to resume writing, there are numerous opinions about how a good resume should look and what it should say. As a result, there is considerable confusion, and the average job seeker does not know what to believe. Chapter 2 sets the record straight! It addresses many of these common myths, explaining why you should not believe them. It also provides a list of resume "do's and don'ts" that serve as an excellent guide when preparing your own resume. It tells you what common pitfalls to avoid, and what things you can do to make your resume far more effective and productive.

Chapter 3, *Resume Prework*, is designed to save you considerable time when it comes time to actually write your resume. This chapter provides a step-by-step process for helping you systematically gather the information you will need. You will then have this information at your fingertips when it comes time to write the actual resume, making the whole process much easier.

A key component of this book, Chapter 4, *Resume Writing: "By the Numbers,"* walks you step-by-step through each section of the resume, giving you detailed instructions and providing excellent examples so you can immediately understand what is needed. To make the process clear, the chapter includes a sample resume containing numbered sections. By reading the numbered instructions provided in the chapter, and then looking at the corresponding numbered section of the sample resume, you will readily understand exactly what to do to create an effective resume document. It is resume writing "by the numbers." It doesn't get any easier than this!

Chapter 5 follows with numerous examples of resumes covering a wide range of hourly paid positions. These sample resumes cover several occupational areas, making it fairly easy for you to find those resumes that most closely relate to your own job-hunting objective. These sample resumes can then be used as the basis for tailoring your own resume, allowing you to borrow from both the ideas and language contained in each.

In addition to needing a resume, you also need to write cover letters. Chapter 6 helps you do this. These cover letters, if well written, can be very effective in convincing an employer to invite you for a job interview. The book covers the two critical types of cover letters you will need:

1. Advertising response cover letters.
2. Employer broadcast letters.

The advertising response cover letter is used to transmit your resume to an employer in response to an Internet or newspaper ad for a position in which you are interested.

The employer broadcast cover letter, on the other hand, is used to send your resume to a large number of employers who may have an interest in your background. You will need both of these letters in order to run an effective job-hunting campaign.

The two final chapters of the book (Chapters 7 and 8) provide detailed instructions for preparing both types of cover letters. Following the same process as Chapter 4 on resume writing, each of these chapters contains a sample cover letter with numbered sections and specific instructions for preparing each section. These detailed, step-by-step instructions are followed by four additional cover letter samples that you can use as templates for writing your own cover letters.

Armed with the careful instructions and advice provided in this book, you have everything you need to write an effective resume and cover letters—the necessary cornerstones on which to build a highly successful job-hunting campaign.

My best wishes to you for a successful job search and a rewarding career.

RICHARD H. BEATTY

West Chester, Pennsylvania

Contents

HOW TO WRITE
A RESUME IF YOU DIDN'T
GO TO COLLEGE

1

Do You Really Need a Resume? Yes!!

It wasn't long ago that hourly paid employees, with few exceptions, did not require an employment resume. When you wanted a job, you simply read the newspaper want ads to find out who was hiring, and then stopped by the employer's plant or office facility and filled out an employment application. Or, alternately, your neighbor, who worked at the employer's facility stopped by the Human Resources department, picked up an application form and brought it home for you to fill out.

Back then the job-hunting process was pretty simple and well defined. You simply visited enough employers' offices, wore some shoe leather down, and filled out tons of employment applications. Sooner or later, if you were lucky and worked hard at the process, you would get a phone call and be off to the job interview. Assuming the interview went well, you then packed your lunch pale or brown bag and started work the next day.

Well, that may have been the way it was a few years ago but, today, the world of job hunting, as you have known it, is changing dramatically and rapidly. As an hourly paid worker, you need to be fully aware of these changes and adapt your job-hunting strategy accordingly. Failure to do so is bound to leave you out in the cold, looking in, and wandering what went wrong.

Let's take a look at how things have changed and what you now need to do differently to be sure that you are on the right track and that your job-hunting campaign will be successful.

THE NEW JOB MARKET

The first thing you need to know about the new job market is that newspaper advertising, the major source of jobs in the past, is now being rapidly replaced by Internet job boards and direct advertising on company Web sites. If you're not particularly computer literate, don't worry, I will show you how to get around this small obstacle a little later on. But, first, you need a clearer understanding of how the job market is changing and what you must do to take full advantage of it.

Why are so many companies now using the Internet to advertise their jobs instead of newspapers? First, Internet advertising is far cheaper. Where a reasonable sized display ad in a newspaper (especially larger newspapers) could easily cost a company $2,000 or more for a single day, an ad on a major Internet job board, such as Monster.com, is likely to cost only a couple hundred dollars or so. And, it will run for 60 days or longer. This is a sizeable difference.

Further, when a company decides to list the job on its own Internet Web site, instead of advertising in a newspaper or on a commercial job board, the cost to the company is zero. That is pretty tough to beat! So, you can easily see why companies are rapidly shifting from newspapers to advertising their job openings on the Internet.

But cost is not the only reason why companies are making the switch. The other is the size of the audience reached. Newspaper ads reach only a local or regional audience of job seekers. Stated differently, ad exposure is generally limited to only those reading that particular newspaper. By contrast, Internet ads reach a global audience. There are no geographical limits, and the audience reading a given ad can be huge. Further, by having the Internet ad run for 60 days or more, as opposed to the typical one-day shot in a local newspaper, employers can expect to receive a substantially greater response than they would ever get from their newspaper!

So, the bottom line is that jobs advertised on the Internet are considerably cheaper and are far more likely to get greater candidate response than those run in newspapers. This being said, it should be obvious (if you are not already doing so) that you will need to refocus your job-hunting efforts away from the newspapers and more toward the Internet. This is not to say you should stop reading the classified want ads entirely. Not so! You will want to continue to read these, but you will also want to focus more and more of your effort on the Internet. It's the place to which the bulk of hourly job advertisement is moving!

WHY YOU NEED A RESUME

If you are going to use the Internet for job-hunting, you are going to need a resume. Most job boards and employer Web sites want you to "paste" a copy of your resume in the space provided for this purpose so they have the opportunity to review your background and qualifications. If you don't already have a resume, you're going to need one, and this book is going to help you develop a really good one!

YOUR KIDS CAN HELP

If you are not comfortable with computers, try your children. Today, most children of school age are quite skilled at using a computer and can teach you a thing or two.

If you don't have children, perhaps you have a niece or nephew who might be willing to give you a hand. You might also try the regional office of your state employment service. Many are well equipped with computers, and there is usually a counselor available who can lend a hand in getting your resume posted on the more popular Internet job boards.

By the way, posting your resume on most major job boards will cost you absolutely nothing. That's about as good a deal as you can find these days. The only thing it will cost is the time it takes to post it. Once posted on the job board Web site, your resume is than stored in a searchable resume database that employers pay a small fee to search. There are now thousands of employers and perhaps millions of recruiters using these resume databases to find qualified candidates for their job openings. So, you'll want your resume to be there!

You will be provided with a list of the most popular Web sites a little later in this book but, for now, let's get back to the subject of resume writing.

OTHER REASONS FOR HAVING A RESUME

Today, we are beginning to see a much greater number of hourly paid workers with resumes. Although certainly spurred on by the rapid growth of the Internet as a job-hunting tool, many hourly paid workers have now also come to realize that having a resume can give them a huge competitive advantage over those who don't. Here are some of these advantages.

1. Speed and Timesaving

Having a resume can be an enormous timesaver. If responding to a newspaper ad, for example, it is much easier and faster to send the employer a resume rather than make a trip to the employer's office to pick up and fill out an employment application. In the time it would take you to go to a single employer's office to pick up an application, you could easily send out a dozen or so resumes to other employers, thus greatly increasing your chances of landing a job interview sooner.

This is doubly true when the employer's ad provides an e-mail address to which your resume can be immediately sent. In such cases, the employer can have your resume in a matter of seconds. You could well be contacted by the employer and scheduled for a job interview before a second candidate, who has not e-mailed his or her resume, has even arrived at the same employer's office to pick up an employment application.

Things can happen fast on the Internet. I know of a case where a job seeker was turned down during a job interview in the morning, returned to his office in the late morning to find an e-mail invitation for a job interview with another company early that same afternoon. By the end of the day, he was offered and accepted that job. Thanks to the Internet, it all happened in a half day. Sometimes, it can be just that quick.

2. The Resume and Job Application—Together, a Great One-Two Punch

Even if planning to physically pick up an employment application, you can realize a significant advantage over other candidates if you attach a copy of your resume to the completed application form when submitting it to the employer. Most employers are likely to be impressed to see that you have invested the time and effort to present them with both. It speaks volumes about the level of your interest in their job and your willingness to go the extra mile to get what you want. It also suggests some very positive things about your commitment and drive—desirable attributes that won't go unnoticed by the employer.

Also, if well designed and carefully written, a good resume will do an effective job of highlighting your key skills and abilities, thereby persuading employers that you are worth bringing in for a job interview. Because of space limitations, this is hard to achieve with just the employment application alone. Thus, in providing the employer with a resume, you are gaining a decided competitive advantage over other candidates who have not taken the time to prepare one.

3. Resumes Contribute to More Effective Interviews

Over the last 15 years, my company, Brandywine Consulting Group, has worked with literally thousands of hourly paid workers who were caught in company downsizings, helping them with their job-hunting process. In doing so we worked with some notable companies, such as Procter & Gamble, Caterpillar Corporation, PepsiCo, Du Pont, and several others.

A few years ago, we began working with hourly paid workers to prepare resumes, something we had never done before. The results were striking. Having a resume not only helped these displaced workers land many more job interviews, but feedback from the workers themselves suggested that the resume preparation process helped them build confidence in their interviewing skills, making them far more effective in the actual interview.

The reason for this is obvious: Taking the time to prepare a resume helps workers better articulate their work experience, skills, and accomplishments during the job interview. It is a kind of "dress rehearsal" for the interview itself, increasing the worker's self-confidence and overall interviewing skills. As a result of having hourly paid workers prepare resumes, my company witnessed a marked improvement in the number of job offers received by the group with resumes when compared to previous groups that had not had the benefit of the resume preparation experience.

Taking the time to write a good resume can have the added benefit of helping you to greatly improve your self-confidence and interviewing effectiveness.

4. The Resume as an Interview Road Map

Often, when the interviewer or hiring manager has a resume, they will use it as a road map of sorts when conducting the employment interview. When this occurs, they typically walk systematically through the resume, one section at a time, from beginning to end.

If well written, the resume emphasizes strengths and attributes, focusing the interviewer's attention on those factors most beneficial to "making the sale." A well-written resume provides the reader with a good understanding of where you've worked and what you've done, leaving more time to discuss your specific skills and attributes—the very things that will heighten the employer's interest in your candidacy, causing you to stand out from other candidates being considered for the job.

5. The Resume as a Comparison Document

The other important role of the resume is to serve as a comparison document. Early in the process, the employer will use the employment application as the basis for comparing candidates in an effort to determine who should be brought in for a job interview. The problem with most employment applications is that they provide only limited information on which to make this judgment. Space constraints of the application form severely limit the amount of information a candidate can provide an employer.

By including a well-written resume along with the employment application, job candidates have the opportunity to provide far more information about their experience, skills, and overall qualifications than can be accommodated on the job application form. A well-designed resume that highlights your knowledge and skills will therefore stack the deck in your favor, increasing the likelihood you will be chosen, from among the masses, to be interviewed for the position.

Having presented you with a convincing case why you are in need of a good resume to greatly increase your chances of job-hunting success, the challenge now is to provide you with an easy-to-follow, step-by-step process to help you prepare an effective resume and realize a significant advantage in today's highly competitive job market. I promise to make this process as painless as possible.

2

Resume Do's and Don'ts

Now that we've established that you will be needing a resume, we need to address some of the commonly held myths about resume writing, of which there are many! Unfortunately, there is a great deal of misinformation out there about what a resume should contain and how it should look. In too many cases these myths are perpetuated by persons having strong opinions about resume writing but have never been on the receiving end of a single resume document. Many have strong opinions on the subject but simply lack the first-hand knowledge and credentials to back it up.

With some people, the less knowledge they have on a subject, the more expert they seem to become. You've heard the old saying that "a little knowledge is dangerous." Well, in the case of resume writing, it can be fatal. This is one subject where it is important to know that you are getting proper advice. The success of your job search depends on it.

So, you need to know that, as this book's author, I have had years of hands-on, practical experience with both reading and preparing resumes. There's nothing like reading thousands-upon-thousands of resumes, as an employer, to gain a deep appreciation and understanding of what makes an outstanding resume or, for that matter, what an awful resume looks like. To reassure you, here is a summary of my extensive experience, both as an employer reading tons of resumes as well as an outplacement consultant who has written thousands of resumes for employees who have been laid off as a result of plant closures and corporate downsizing. If experience counts, you might consider me a "resume Olympian" of sorts! I have run the equivalent of numerous resume marathons. My training has been both rigorous and complete.

During earlier years, I was a human resources manager for a number of Scott Paper Company manufacturing plants, where I interviewed and hired hundreds of hourly paid workers for a wide range of positions. Later, while working in the company's corporate employment function for nearly seven years, I provided recruiting and employment support to the company's corporate offices as well as 13 manufacturing plants. This included staffing a $1.5 billion company expansion. My Scott Paper experience was then followed by over 18 years in the consulting business where I provided recruiting and interviewing support to a number of companies across a wide range of industries. This consulting has included several projects requiring the hiring of hundreds of persons to staff new and/or expanding operations.

None of this is intended to impress you. It's only to let you know that I have done an enormous amount of hiring of hourly paid workers and have had to read stacks-upon-stacks of resumes in order to do so. In fact, my best estimate is that I have personally read in excess of 200,000 resumes during my career as both a human resources professional and employment consultant. This may well be the reason why I now wear such thick glasses!

I think you can well imagine, with my having read such a huge volume of resumes over the years, that I now have a solid understanding of what is required to produce an effective resume document. Further, through this same practical experience, I have come to learn what impresses an employer in a resume document and what does not. I have come to appreciate why certain resumes will motivate an employer to bring some candidates in for a job interview but turn others away.

You might also be interested to know that during the last 15 years, while running Brandywine Consulting Group, I have contracted with a number of large corporations to provide them with outplacement consulting services. These projects involved working with thousands of hourly paid and salaried workers who had lost their jobs as a result of corporate downsizings and plant shutdowns. Some of these projects have required us to run outplacement centers for several months, helping displaced workers conduct an effective job search including the preparation of resume documents tailored to their specific employment needs.

Over the years, we have worked with thousands of such workers and had the opportunity to experiment with a number of different resume types and styles. Over time, this experimentation has enabled us to continuously fine-tune our approach to the point that we now have arrived at a specific resume design that has consistently proven to be highly effective. Workers, going through our programs, in fact, frequently comment on just how helpful their resume has been and have also passed along the many favorable remarks employers have made about the quality of their resumes during job interviews.

Enough said on my background and experience. Let's now move on to commonly held resume myths, and some of the important do's and don'ts of which you will want to be aware when writing your resume.

COMMON RESUME MYTHS

Myth #1: Don't include a "job objective" on your resume.

Those who would have you believe your resume should exclude a job objective, argue that it could screen you out from other positions in which you might have interest. They would tell you that in leaving the job objective off the resume, the field is wide open and the employer will want to look at your qualifications for a number of job openings, thus increasing the chances of your getting a job interview.

Although this argument sounds logical on the surface, there is a stronger counter argument for including an objective statement on your resume. A recent survey of nearly 600 employers showed that including a objective statement on the resume was felt to be important to very important.

The reason behind the employer's preference has to do with the number of resumes they must read. Many employers are required to read thousands of resumes a year. Consequently, if the resume doesn't clearly show the kind of job you are seeking, they are likely to move on to one that does. The last thing the employer wants to do is to read through an entire resume and guess at the type of job you are seeking. Employers are simply too busy and won't waste the time.

Myth #2: *Resumes should never be more than one page in length.*

Although it is true that a recent high school graduate or a person with only a couple years of experience should limit their resume to a single page, this is not the case with those having extensive experience. In such cases, a well-written resume requires at least a page and a half, if not a full two pages.

Clearly, you don't want to try and cram 10 or 15 years of experience on to a single-page resume. This is especially true if, in doing so, the resume becomes crowded and difficult to read. This is also true if forcing your experience into a single-page document causes you to exclude important experience or skills that you possess.

If you still have reservations about having your resume spill over on to a second page, you might want to consider this fact: A survey of nearly 600 human resource professionals showed that 91 percent felt a two-page resume was quite acceptable.

There are some good reasons for these survey results. First, use of a two-page resume allows you to leave more white space between resume sections, making the resume easier to read. Take a look at some of the sample resumes shown in this book, and you'll see exactly what I mean. If you tried to cram the same amount of information on to a single page, chances are the resume would look cramped and would be difficult to read. The easier you make it for the employer to read your resume, the greater is the likelihood that it will, in fact, be read!

Additionally, a well-written two-page resume can provide the employer with more information about your skills, competencies, and experience. It presents a more complete picture of your overall qualifications and, in most cases, enhances the likelihood of capturing the employer's interest.

Myth #3: *Long resumes do a better job of attracting the employer's interest.*

Only in rare cases should a job resume be more than two pages in length. You can overdo it and turn employers off if your resume is too long or too detailed.

Over the years, I have seen some pretty long resumes. One stands out in particular. This resume was over 20 pages long and was bound in a cover. This was not a resume—it was a book! Did I read it? No way! I wasn't about to waste my time weeding through 20 pages of resume. I only needed the highlights, not the candidate's life story.

My view on lengthy resumes seems to be shared by the majority of employers. One employer survey I've seen showed that 62 percent of employers objected to resumes that were longer than two pages. This supports the idea that resumes, with very rare exception, should never be longer than two pages.

Myth #4: Your resume's appearance needs to be different so it stands out from others and grabs the employer's attention.

I've seen them all. I've seen resumes on pink or chartreuse paper, resumes with pop-up parts, resumes handwritten on a postcard, a resume folded up inside of a pill case (the candidate had designed the pill box), even one resume printed on toilet paper (I was working for a paper company at the time). In one case, the candidate even included a dollar bill suggesting I go get a cup of coffee while I read his resume.

Unique or unusual resumes of this type, although well intended, should be avoided. They can often backfire.

Although you may succeed in getting the employer's attention, many employers will begin wondering about your motivation for taking such an unusual approach. For instance, does this resume suggest you are a person that needs to be the center of attention? If so, what kind of a team player would you be? Does the fact that you chose to use this kind of gimmick approach suggest you are non-conventional—a bit of a rebel? If so, does this mean you might be a difficult person to manage? Or, finally, does using this kind of unusual approach suggest you are someone who is ignorant about commonly accepted employment application behavior?

As you can see, using unusual or outlandish resumes to attract attention may get the employer's attention, but it may not be the kind of attention you would like. It can raise far more questions than it provides answers to, causing employers to shy away rather than be interested in you.

My best advice is—don't resort to using gimmick resumes. Stick with conventional approaches. It will raise far fewer eyebrows and enhance your employment chances.

Myth #5: Don't worry about how your resume looks. It's much more important that it says the right things.

The terms we use to describe how a resume physically looks is what we call *format* or *resume design*. Although having the right information in the resume is certainly important, it is equally important to have a resume that is well formatted.

A poorly formatted resume is usually difficult to read. If the resume sections are crowded together without much white space in between, or if there are no distinct section headings that visually separate one resume section from another, the resume will be far more difficult to read. Not only will it take the employer more time to read the resume, but lack of proper headings and poor layout will make it far more difficult for the employer to find the information needed to make an employment decision.

Obviously, you don't want to create these kinds of problems for the employer. These problems encourage the employer to skip your resume entirely and move right on to the next one.

Take a look at the sample resumes presented later in this book and note how they are formatted and designed. Notice, in particular, how white space and resume headings are used to separate the various resume sections. See how easy it is to read the resume and find important information quickly.

In Chapter 4, *Resume Writing: "By the Numbers,"* I will provide you with easy-to-follow instructions on how to properly format a resume so that it is easy for employers to read.

Myth #6: *Always include references on your resume.*

Although it used to be the thing to do, it is no longer correct to list references on your job resume. They waste valuable space that could be better used to describe your job experience, skills, and talents. The employer just doesn't need references at this point and they just clutter up the resume with information that has little use at this stage of the process.

Over the years, I have seen cases where premature disclosure of references on the resume caused a problem. In these cases, the employer decided to contact a few references before inviting the job seeker in for interviews, and the reference check backfired. Thus, the candidate never had the opportunity to interview for the job. They never even got through the front door.

The slightest bit of negative information provided by a reference is often all it takes for an employer to decide not to proceed with the interview. The story can be quite different if the interview goes particularly well, and the employer is impressed with your qualifications. In those cases, the positive impression created during the interview can more than offset a slightly negative reference. If you are screened out without the chance to interview, however, you never even get a shot at the job.

So, bottom line—don't provide references on your resume. Take a list of references along to the interview, however, don't volunteer them unless the employer asks for them. If they are interested in you at the conclusion of the interview, and feel they need to check references, they will ask you for them.

Myth #7: *Lie or exaggerate on your resume. Nobody ever checks anyway.*

This is clearly not a good idea and could well cost you the job offer. Putting aside the likelihood that your lie or exaggeration could be uncovered during a reference check, you could also be "found out" during the interview itself. Nothing can be more embarrassing or kill an interview faster. I have seen it happen!

A skillful interviewer will employ specific techniques designed to uncover exaggerations or lies during the interview process. When using one such technique, known as *patterning,* for example, the interviewer will ask the same question (but slightly disguised) more than once during the interview to check the consistency and honesty of your answers.

For example, if your resume states that you are a strong team player, and this trait is important, the employer may elect to use the interview to test your honesty. The interviewer, for example, might ask you a couple of questions (at different times during the interview) to check your honesty. In one case, the interviewer might ask you to describe a time when you disagreed with a couple of your coworkers and then ask what you did about it. Later in the interview, the interviewer may attempt to get a fix on just how good a team player you are by asking you to describe a time when you did not particularly enjoy working with a group of people with whom you had to work.

Both of these questions are designed to test how well you get along with fellow workers and how well you manage conflict with others. A good team player finds ways to work through difficulties with others and build strong working relationships. Obviously a misstep in answering either of these questions is going to raise serious doubts about your resume statement where you indicated you are a "strong team player."

I think you can readily see, from the example just cited, that it's not a good idea to lie or exaggerate on your resume. Sooner or later it can come back to haunt you. Honesty is truly the best policy. Keep your resume factual and honest.

Myth #8: *You need to list personal data (such as height, weight, marital status) on your resume.*

To the contrary, you do *not* want to list personal data on your resume. Today's resumes specifically exclude such information, and for good reason.

First, it is illegal for an employer to discriminate against a job candidate on the basis of age, sex, race, creed, color, national origin, or physical handicap. So, employers don't want to see this kind of personal information on the resume. Second, if you decided to list this kind of information on your job resume, it may be illegally used to discriminate against you and screen you out from further employment consideration. And, finally, since it is a well-known fact that this kind of information no longer has a place on the resume, it may cause the employer to question just how up-to-date you are about what is going on in the world.

So, don't list personal data on the resume. It could prove to be the thing that causes an employer to discard your resume and move on to the next employment candidate.

Myth #9: *Hobbies and outside activities should be shown on the resume.*

At one time, listing outside hobbies and extracurricular activities on the resume was thought to be a good thing to do. It was believed that employers preferred candidates who were "well rounded," those who were active in their communities and had a multitude of interests. Such activities were believed to suggest to employers that the candidate was productive, motivated, high-energy, responsible, or had other similar traits considered desirable.

The trend today, however, is to exclude hobbies and outside activities from the resume entirely, unless they are "job relevant." By "job relevant," it is meant that these activities specifically demonstrate that you have certain knowledge or skills directly related to performing the job for which you are applying. Otherwise, listing these activities simply takes up valuable resume space that could be better used to describe work experience or skills that are truly important to performing the job.

As you can see, there are many resume myths still out there. People continue to perpetuate these myths and we continue to see the same old mistakes on resumes, time-and-time-again! This is really unfortunate since the average job seeker has no idea what to believe and therefore can end up, with perfectly good intentions, doing something that can have a very negative impact on their job-hunting efforts.

Now that we've dispelled some of the common myths about resume preparation, let's take a look at some of the resume dos and don'ts you need to be aware of. These guidelines should help you avoid some of the common resume mistakes and make sure you end up creating a resume that will serve you well throughout the job search process.

RESUME DO'S AND DON'TS

1. Use white or off-white paper of good quality (20 pound weight, or better).
2. Avoid use of colored paper, such as grays, blues, greens, and so on. This can be distracting and make it difficult to read or scan the resume by computer.
3. Use standard 8½″ × 11″ paper, avoiding legal or other nonstandard sizes. Make good use of white space so things are not crowded and your resume is easy for employers to read.
4. Pay particular attention to the neatness of your resume. Make sure there are no ragged margins, and that the text is well organized and visually pleasing.
5. If you are not an experienced typist, consider having a professional typing service prepare your resume for you. It may be well worth the $25 or so that you'll spend.
6. Use common business typefaces such as Courier, Times Roman, Helvetica, Times New Roman, Arial, or Palatino. Use of unusual typefaces may make it difficult for employers to scan or use a computer to search your resume.
7. Use 12-point font size, although 10- and 14-point are normally acceptable.
8. Avoid underlining, shading, pictures, or graphics of any kind because these may interfere with computer scanning or resume keyword search. Keep it simple; stick with text only.
9. Make sure typing or printing is neat and crisp, not blurred or fuzzy in any way. Use of a laser jet or modern ink jet printer is desirable when printing the resume.

10. Follow standard resume formats (as described in this book). Avoid any unusual, unique, or nonstandard resume layouts.

11. Avoid "gimmick resumes" (unusual resumes designed as attention getters). These can be somewhat annoying and leave the employer with a negative rather than the positive reaction they were intended to create. Stick with conventional design and approaches.

12. Keep resumes to a reasonable length. A single page should be ample for someone with only a couple years experience. A two-page resume is quite acceptable for persons with five or more years of experience. If at all possible, however, avoid using more than two pages.

13. Avoid spelling errors or obvious grammatical mistakes. If you are not good at spelling or grammar, have someone else read your resume who is skilled in these areas. Never send your resume to an employer without at least one other person proofreading it. It is often difficult to spot your own mistakes, and you will likely overlook them.

14. Always include an objective statement, so employers know the type of job you are seeking.

15. In almost all cases, you will want to use a reverse chronological style resume. This style resume starts with your current or most recent job first, and then presents past jobs in reverse order starting with your next most recent job and ending with your first job. (This book will show you how to prepare this type of resume.)

16. Follow your objective statement with a summary section that highlights your key skills, competencies, and personal attributes. Employers using computers and keyword search to identify candidates will often focus on this section of the resume to identify persons with certain skill sets and personal attributes important to job success.

17. Do not lie or misrepresent your qualifications and experience. An experienced interviewer could well discover this indiscretion causing considerable embarrassment and destroying your opportunity for employment. A check of your references may also prove disastrous, if you have been less than truthful with the employer.

18. Do not list personal data such as age, weight, height, health, race, religious affiliation, or marital status on the resume. Employers could use this information to illegally discriminate against you. The modern resume excludes this type of personal information as it is considered not to be job relevant.

19. Include a list of company-sponsored training programs you have attended and professional licenses and/or certifications you have earned. These can serve to provide a competitive advantage over other employment candidates with whom you are competing, as well as signaling prospective employers that you are motivated to continuously upgrade your knowledge and skills.

20. Do not include references on your resume, as the modern resume specifically excludes them. If the employer wants references, they will ask for them.

21. Do not include hobbies or extra-curricular activities on the resume unless they are directly related to the type of position you are seeking. Listing hobbies or extracurricular activities is an old-fashioned practice that no longer has a place in modern resume design.

By now you should have a good understanding of a number of common resume myths as well as a good comprehension of some key resume do's and don'ts pertaining to the writing of an effective resume. It is now time to begin the process of organizing the information you will need to actually write the resume itself.

3

Resume Prework: Getting Ready to Write

If you are feeling a bit anxious about being able to write an effective resume—relax, you have a lot of company. Writing a resume is something most people find difficult to do. I have seen bright, well-educated, articulate corporate executives struggle when it came time to reduce their experience and credentials to a two-page resume document. Despite all their education and qualifications, many find it a difficult thing to do. This is an absolutely normal reaction at this stage, but you are about to find out that writing a resume is going to be much easier than you thought.

This chapter will help you overcome some of these initial resume writing jitters and will lead you through the preparation process one step at a time. It's like that old saying, "How do you eat an elephant?" The answer: "One bite at a time!" So, we are going to eat this elephant together—one bite at a time!

CALMING YOUR FEARS

When trying to quell your doubts and uneasiness about resume writing, a little common sense and reasoning can go a long way. Generally speaking, most people fear what they don't know. Therefore, if you have never written a resume, this may seem like the equivalent of attempting to climb Mount Everest. You just don't know what to expect.

When it comes to writing a resume, much of the uneasiness is caused by lack of knowledge in one or more of the following categories:

1. Resume content (What do I say or not say?)
2. Resume format (How should I organize it? What do I say first, second, etc.?)
3. Resume style (How do I best say it?)

If you know what to say, in what order it should be said, and how you should say it, there's not much else to be concerned about. In addition, the more you have prepared, organized, and rehearsed, the more comfortable you will be in your ability to write a really good resume. This chapter is designed to help you develop these resume-preparation skills and the confidence to move on to the actual writing process.

This chapter helps you in two areas. First, it helps you systematically collect and organize all of the information you will need to write your resume. Second, it helps you with your writing style. It shows you not just what to say, but how to say it. Don't worry if you don't consider yourself a very good writer. This is going to be much easier than you might think.

Here we go! Let's take that first bite of the elephant.

COLLECTING AND ORGANIZING RESUME FACTS

As with most complex tasks, the need for planning and good organization is essential. Resume writing is no exception.

Before you can proceed to actually write your resume, you first need to collect and systematically organize the basic facts that you will need to have at your fingertips when you begin to actually write. Moreover, these facts need to be organized in the proper sequence so that they will be available in the order that you will need them.

The following forms are designed to help you systematically collect and organize this information. Take your time and carefully fill them out. Doing so is going to save you considerable time and avoid much frustration when it is time to begin the process of actually writing your resume.

YOUR JOB OBJECTIVE

In simple terms, describe the type of job for which you will be looking:

Objective: _____

_____

Here are a few examples of job-hunting objectives to get you started. For some further ideas on how to word your objective, take a look at some of the objectives shown on the several resume samples provided in this book. If you are not sure what to write, a simple job title will do just fine.

Objective: Administrative Assistant in a Corporate Office Environment

Objective: Machine Operator or Production Worker

Objective: Instrument Repair Technician

Objective: Shipping and Receiving Clerk

Objective: Forklift Truck Operator/Warehouse Worker

Objective: Quality Control TechnicianPharmaceutical or Chemical Process Company

Do you have a secondary job objective? If so, write it in the space provided below:

Secondary Objective: _____

_____

Sometimes, if the secondary objective is closely related to your primary objective, you can combine the two. For example:

Objective: Hourly Leader or Machine Operator in a Manufacturing Plant

Objective: Electrician or Instrument Repair Technician

Objective: Legal Secretary/Entry-Level Paralegal

WORK EXPERIENCE

In this section, starting with your current job or most recent position, list all of the employers for whom you have worked during your career. Record dates of employment, employer's name, name of the department or function in which you worked, title of the job you held, title of the person to whom you reported, and your principal job duties. If you get stuck describing your job duties, find some similar sample resumes in this book and carefully study how job duties were described. In doing so, you will quickly see how to do it.

In those cases where you have held more than one position with the same employer, write the word "same" in the space provided for the employer's name.

In the case where multiple jobs were held with the same employer, continue to list them in reverse chronological order (starting with the most recently held position first) and list the dates you held these jobs in the "Dates Employed" section. These then become the dates you were employed in each specific position.

Use each of the pages provided to list a single job. Try to be as thorough as possible in describing your job duties. Again, if you get stuck in describing these, look at the job descriptions contained in the sample resumes. The sample resumes should give you an excellent idea of how to describe these duties.

Job # 1 (Current or Most Recent Job)

Dates Employed: From: _____   To: _____

Employer: _____

Department or Function: _____

Boss' Title: _____

Your Job Title: _____

Job Duties: _____

_____

_____

_____

_____

_____

_____

_____

_____

_____

_____

_____

_____

_____

_____

_____

_____

Job # 2 (Next Most Recent Job)

Dates Employed: From: _____   To: _____

Employer: _____

Department or Function: _____

Boss' Title: _____

Your Job Title: _____

Job Duties: _____

_____

_____

_____

_____

_____

_____

_____

_____

_____

_____

_____

_____

_____

_____

_____

Job # 3 (Next Most Recent Job)

Dates Employed: From: _____   To: _____

Employer: _____

Department or Function: _____

Boss' Title: _____

Your Job Title: _____

Job Duties: _____

_____

_____

_____

_____

_____

_____

_____

_____

_____

_____

_____

_____

_____

_____

_____

Job # 4 (Next Most Recent Job)

Dates Employed: From: _____   To: _____

Employer: _____

Department or Function: _____

Boss' Title: _____

Your Job Title: _____

Job Duties: _____

_____

_____

_____

_____

_____

_____

_____

_____

_____

_____

_____

_____

_____

_____

_____

_____

Job # 5 (Next Most Recent Job)

Dates Employed: From: _____   To: _____

Employer: _____

Department or Function: _____

Boss' Title: _____

Your Job Title: _____

Job Duties: _____

_____

_____

_____

_____

_____

_____

_____

_____

_____

_____

_____

_____

_____

_____

_____

_____

Job # 6 (Next Most Recent Job)

Dates Employed: From: _____   To: _____

Employer: _____

Department or Function: _____

Boss' Title: _____

Your Job Title: _____

Job Duties: _____

_____

_____

_____

_____

_____

_____

_____

_____

_____

_____

_____

_____

_____

_____

_____

_____

Job # 7 (Next Most Recent Job)

Dates Employed: From: _____   To: _____

Employer: _____

Department or Function: _____

Boss' Title: _____

Your Job Title: _____

Job Duties: _____

_____

_____

_____

_____

_____

_____

_____

_____

_____

_____

_____

_____

_____

_____

_____

Job # 8 (Current or Most Recent Job)

Dates Employed: From: _____   To: _____

Employer: _____

Department or Function: _____

Boss' Title: _____

Your Job Title: _____

Job Duties: _____

_____

_____

_____

_____

_____

_____

_____

_____

_____

_____

_____

_____

_____

_____

_____

_____

_____

EDUCATION

In this section, list your formal education, such as high school diploma, trade school diploma, associates degree, and so on. If you graduated from a trade school or earned an associates degree, show your major or field of study. Also, show any special honors or awards you received in recognition of your school achievements. Do not list company training here. It should be listed in the next section.

Diploma: Yes or No? _____

School Name: _____

Major/Field of Study: _____

Graduation Date: _____

Honors or Awards: _____

_____

Diploma: Yes or No? _____

School Name: _____

Major/Field of Study: _____

Graduation Date: _____

Honors or Awards: _____

_____

Dates Attended (if did not graduate):   **From:** _____   **To:** _____

Company-Sponsored and/or Other Training

List any company-sponsored or other relevant training you have had. List only those programs related to the type of job you are seeking or that may be important for an employer to know about (such as safety training). See sample resumes for types of training programs normally listed in this section.

Name of Program or Course	Date Completed	Company Sponsored? (Yes) (No)
_____	_____	_____
_____	_____	_____
_____	_____	_____
_____	_____	_____
_____	_____	_____
_____	_____	_____

Licenses and Certificates

Record any special licenses or certificates that you have earned that are related to the type of work you are seeking. This includes professional licenses issued by state or local government agencies, as well as certificates you have been awarded as the result of completion of special training related to your occupation and job interests.

Name of License/ Certificate	Issuing School or Authority	Date Awarded
_____	_____	_____
_____	_____	_____
_____	_____	_____
_____	_____	_____
_____	_____	_____

Computer-Related Skills (Hardware/Software)

With the importance of computers in so many jobs today, it is a good idea to list any computer skills, both hardware and software, you may have. As a machine operator, you may have had to use control systems, for example. If so, list the types of control systems you have operated.

Hardware: (Including Control Systems)

_____

_____

_____

_____

_____

_____

_____

Software:

_____

_____

_____

_____

_____

_____

_____

_____

_____

Special Tools and Equipment

Are you qualified or skilled at using any special tools and equipment normally required in the type of job for which you are applying? This could include machinery, hand tools, power tools, testing instruments, vehicles, cranes, and the like. If so, list them in the space provided:

_____

_____

_____

_____

_____

_____

If you have completed the worksheets contained in this chapter, you are more than half way through the resume writing process. As you will see in the next chapter, all of this hard work will pay off handsomely. It is now simply a matter of plugging this information into the right resume format or layout, which is what we will be doing in the next chapter, *Resume Writing: "By the Numbers."* It doesn't get much simpler than this!

4

Resume Writing: "By the Numbers"

In the last chapter, we systematically collected the basic information you will need to write your resume. As you will quickly learn, this information will now prove quite useful as we begin to help you prepare the actual resume document. I know, from working with thousands of others in writing effective resumes, that the work you did in Chapter 3 is going to save considerable time enabling you to directly plug much of this information into the resume format or layout we will be discussing here in this chapter.

You will notice that the heading of this chapter includes the words "by the numbers." Rather than simply providing a broad discussion of the resume and its various components, we are going to walk you systematically through each resume section literally "by the numbers."

A glance at the resume sample on the next two pages will show you that each resume component has a number. To make resume writing easier, I will walk you through each resume section, one number at a time. In each case, you will be provided with a detailed description of what that section should include and exactly how it should be written.

To make this process as easy as possible, I strongly recommend that you follow the steps listed:

1. *Study the sample resume.*

Before reading the description of a numbered section, take a moment or two to study that section on the actual sample resume itself. This will permit you to better visualize and understand the recommendations being made in the description of that section in the step-by-step instructions.

WILLIAM B. DAVIS

1

816 Cody Road
Albany, NY 12349

Home: (503) 644-9212   Email: WilDav81@AOL.com   Cell: (206) 752-1238

OBJECTIVE

2

Line Mechanic – Manufacturing & Packaging

SUMMARY

3

Skilled, efficient, hard-working production mechanic with extensive experience in the installation and start-up of new packaging line equipment, including operator training, safety, reliability, and ergonomics. Motivated, self-starter who learns quickly and functions effectively in a team environment. Strong technical contributor with good communications and interpersonal skills.

EXPERIENCE

4

MASON PRODUCTS, INC., Albany, NY   **2000 to Present**
This 450-employee plant manufactures a wide range of household products including cleansers, dishwashing detergents, floor polishes, window cleaners, and other consumer cleaning agents.

5

Line Mechanic – Packaging Operations
Report to Packaging Line Supervisor with responsibility for providing timely mechanical maintenance, troubleshooting, and repair to support the efficient, continuous running of packaging line equipment and minimize line downtime.

- Function as shift mechanic for a 20-employee, 4 machine household products packaging line operation.
- Provide immediate mechanical, on-the-fly troubleshooting support in an effort to maintain continuous line operation and limit machine downtime.
- Served as key member of start-up team, responsible for the successful installation, start-up, and debugging of a $ 5 MM household cleaners packaging line.
- Implemented and maintained machine centerline used to achieve quick product changeovers and reduce need for fine-tuning.

6

- Improved functioning of line equipment to meet rapid changeover demands.
- Reduced unscheduled downtime from 3 hours to 15 minutes per shift through use of downtime tracking system, equipment modification, and creative teaming with equipment vendor.
- Used troubleshooting skills and creative approaches to increase process reliability from 75% to 90% in three-month period.
- Designed and implemented area maintenance systems that were subsequently adopted as the model for all plant packaging lines.
- Assisted in the construction and start-up of new window cleaner packaging line including commissioning, production qualification, and final manufacturing acceptance.
- Consistently met and exceeded line process and efficiency goals through implementation of creative product change methods, and training of line operators in basic maintenance and troubleshooting techniques.

PACKCO EQUIPMENT COMPANY, Utica, NY   **1996 - 2000**
Manufacturer of custom packaging equipment for use in the packaging of a wide range of consumer and commercial products. Equipment includes filling machines, capping equipment, poly-wrap machines, case packers, and sealing equipment.

Packaging Mechanic
Reported to Project Engineer or Senior Project Engineer with responsibility for installation, start-up, debugging, and fine-tuning of new packaging line installations at customer manufacturing facilities.

- Set-up and debugged packaging equipment installations.
- Trained customer employees in equipment operation and maintenance.
- Provided emergency troubleshooting and repair services to customers as needed.
- Member of start-up team responsible for the successful installation and start-up of a $ 10 MM, fully-integrated, continuous packaging line at Procter & Gamble's Nashville plant.
- Appointed chief project mechanic for the case packing and sealing section of a $ 4 million packaging line installation at Johnson & Johnson's Landisville, New Jersey plant.

7	**EDUCATION**

High School Diploma
Utica High School, 1994

Albany Technical Institute, 1995
Courses: Machine Design
          Mechanical Drafting
          Basic Mechanics
          Troubleshooting & Repair

8	**COMPANY TRAINING**

Centerline Quick Changeover
Vendor Machine Training
Video Jet Coders
Honeywell Basic Control Systems
Preventive Maintenance
OSHA Compliance

9	**COMPUTER SKILLS**

Honeywell TDC 3000 Control Systems

2. *Read the description of the numbered section.*

Carefully read the description for the numbered section. Note the specific recommendations made concerning both the physical layout of the section as well as its recommended content.

3. *Restudy the sample resume.*

Again study the sample resume. See how the recommendations made in the section description are actually applied in the resume itself.

4. *Draft your resume section.*

While the instructions are fresh in your mind, and using the sample resume as a guide, next either handwrite or type this section of your own resume.

Note: At this point, you will likely find it extremely helpful to locate a resume that closely resembles the type of job you are seeking from among the numerous resume samples provided in this book. Thus, whether you are a Senior Administrative Assistant, a Forklift Truck Operator, Packing Machine Operator, a Laboratory Technician, or other type worker, you should be able to find a resume sample similar to the type of job you are seeking. This will provide considerable help to you in seeing how to describe such things as job duties and accomplishments.

A STRONG RECOMMENDATION—BEFORE YOU START

Eat this elephant—one bite at a time! As you can see this is a rather lengthy chapter containing several pages that are chocked full with very important information. Don't try to read this whole chapter in a single sitting. That is why the chapter is broken down into numbered sections, each corresponding to its identical number as shown on the sample resume.

Instead, the resume writing process should be spread out over a 3- or 4-day period. This will allow you to eat only a "bite or two" at a time. Try doing only one or two of the numbered sections a day, and focus on doing them very well. You will find, in taking this advice, that the whole process will go much easier for you and the resume you create will end up being a much more effective document than if you tried to do it all in a single day or evening. There is too much information provided in this chapter to tackle it in a single day. If you try to do so, you may find yourself feeling somewhat frustrated and a bit overwhelmed.

Having helped hundreds of persons write resumes, I can tell you from practical experience that very few people can write an effective resume in a single day. You should really not attempt to do this, unless you have no choice. By spreading it out over a few days, you will be far less frustrated and end up with a much better resume to show for your efforts.

If you are not a very good writer (and many people aren't, so don't be embarrassed), this is the time to line up some help. Seek out a relative or friend who you know can write well and ask them to help you. If you are unemployed, you might also seek writing help from a counselor at a State Employment Service. It would probably be a good idea to have them read this chapter first, however, before you get started working together. They will find that helping you will go a lot easier for them if they do, and you will end up with a much better resume then if they have no understanding of what you are attempting to accomplish.

Although it is always easier to have someone else do the work for you, it is an excellent idea for you to try to write at least the initial draft of your resume yourself. This will save considerable time when you meet with your helper. This way, they can simply take what you have written and revise it, rather than having to write everything "from scratch."

Of equal or perhaps greater importance is that by forcing yourself to write the resume yourself, with little or no assistance from others, you will be much better prepared for job interviewers. Forcing yourself to at least write a rough draft of your resume will help you formulate, in your mind, the right words for use in the interview when it comes time to describe your specific job duties and accomplishments to an employer. From my extensive outplacement and career counseling experience, I know for a fact that those employees who struggled to write their own resumes (rather than rely on someone else to do it for them), almost always did much better in the job interview. They are just much better prepared than those who did not.

If writing is not your strength, do as much as you can by yourself, but then get some help from someone who has good writing skills. When you send your resume to an employer, you want to be sure you are putting your best foot forward. It is always a good idea for someone else to carefully look over your resume before you send it to an employer. It is frequently more difficult to spot our own mistakes than it is for others to see them.

Some General Observations

Before starting a detailed description of the various resume sections, it is useful to make a few observations about the general design and layout of the numbered resume sample contained in this chapter. There are several physical features that are important for you to observe and which contribute substantially to the readability and overall effectiveness of the resume document.

Note, first of all, that each of the major resume sections (such as OBJECTIVE, SUMMARY, EXPERIENCE, etc.) are in bold type and use all capital letters. This treatment, along with spacing between each of these key sections, visually sets that section apart from the next section, making it easy for someone reading the resume to quickly locate the key information they are seeking. To further separate these sections, these section headings are set in slightly larger type (12-point) than the text or actual wording contained in each of these sections. The text, by contrast, is set in 11-point type.

If you don't understand what is meant by 12-point or 11-point type, look at the sample resumes provided. You can also use a professional typist or secretarial service who will better understand these instructions, and they will type your resume following these directions. To locate a local typing service that can help you, use the Yellow Pages of your telephone book and look under "Secretarial Services." You will find them listed.

If you decide to use a secretarial service to type your resume, please be cautious because many offer resume preparation services and will try to convince you to pay them a fee to write your resume for you. This may be somewhat tempting, however, I would strongly caution you against doing this. Although some may be quite professional, there are many more that don't have the slightest idea of what a good resume should look like.

I have seen many of the resumes prepared by these services, and I can tell you that although the typing may be very professional, the final resumes (layout and content) can often be absolutely awful. You would be far better off following the instructions in this book, preparing a handwritten resume and then having them type from your handwritten document. In doing so, you might want to show them the sample resume from this chapter as a guide for typing your resume. This will give them a much better understanding of how the final product needs to look.

Returning to the sample resume, you will want to take note of the effective use of white space between each section of the resume. By not crowding or bunching up the sections, one against the other, it makes it far easier for someone to read the resume and to locate the specific information they are seeking. It takes a lot more effort and concentration for an employer to read a resume that is crowded, and many won't even bother. They will simply move on to the next resume.

In viewing the sample resume in this chapter, you will also note that I have carefully avoided the use of underlining, italics, or unusual letters and text. This is very important, since an increasing number of employers are now using computers to electronically read and scan resumes.

Many computer systems use a keyword search to scan resumes, wherein the computer scans hundreds or thousands of employment resumes looking for certain key words that the employer has chosen to identify candidates for a given job. Depending on the scanning software being used by the employer in performing such keyword searches, the computer may not be able to read words that are underlined, written in italics, or make use of an unusual or out-of-the-ordinary typeface or font.

Although the use of capital letters and bold type are acceptable and can now be read by the majority of resume scanning software, you will definitely want to avoid using any underlining, unusual typeface, graphics, charts, and so forth in your resume. Additionally, you should use common business typefaces such as Courier, Times Roman, New Times Roman, Helvetica, or Arial. These are common typefaces that most computer software can read. Doing so will ensure that you will not be eliminated from a job you want just because the computer is unable to read your resume.

We are now ready to help you start writing your resume. We will systematically work through each section of the resume, one number at a time, using the sample resume contained in this chapter as our guide.

1 Resume Heading

The resume heading, labeled as #1 on the sample resume, contains the following basic information: name, address, phone number(s), and e-mail address.

The name and address should be centered on the paper, as shown on the resume sample. You will want your name to stand out, so it should use bold print and should be in a slightly larger type size (12-point) from the address, phone number, and e-mail address (which are set in 11-point type). Capital letters have been used for the name. This treatment makes your name stand out, and makes it easy for an employer to quickly locate your resume if they are looking for it in a stack of resumes.

The address, as you can see from the resume sample, is set in the smaller 11-point type and is centered directly below your name. It should include street address, town or city, state, and zip code. Additionally, this information should be typed using normal rather than bold type.

In our sample resume, we show a candidate who wishes to list a home phone number, a cell phone number, and an e-mail address. Not everyone has a cell phone or e-mail address. If you do not, simply list your home phone number on the next line directly below your address (without a space between the address and phone number). Also, if you wish to show only a home phone number and an e-mail address, then center the e-mail address on the next line directly following your home phone number.

If any of these directions are confusing to you, take a look at the sample resumes provided later in this book. You will quickly see exactly where this information has been placed. When listing two phone numbers and an e-mail address, as shown on this chapter's sample resume, it is a good idea to skip a line after the address and then insert the two phone numbers and e-mail address as shown.

If you do not have a cell phone, you may wish to include a work phone number instead. If you do this, however, make sure that you can take phone calls from potential future employers without being overheard.

Having an e-mail address is becoming increasingly important since, for many employers, e-mail is fast becoming the preferred means of communication. This is becoming increasingly true as more and more of the advertising for hourly paid positions (including laborers and production workers) is now being done on the Internet. As explained earlier, advertising jobs on Internet job boards (like Monster.com, HotJobs, etc.) and the employer's own Web site is much less expensive than continuing to run these ads in the newspaper. Also, studies show that employers feel they get a better quality of candidate from the Internet than they do from traditional newspaper advertising.

If you are not computer literate and don't know how to use the computer, I strongly suggest that you learn to use one. Perhaps you can take a night school at your local high school or at one of the major computer stores such as CompUSA. Having a computer and an Internet connection, along with your own e-mail address, is becoming more and more important to conducting a job search. Maybe now is the time to bite the bullet and learn this skill.

If a computer is not in your future and you have no way to learn how to use one, it would still be a good idea to have an e-mail address. A computer literate child, relative, or close friend can probably help you. If they subscribe to an Internet service, many such services will allow the subscriber to set up more than one e-mail address. Perhaps they could set one up for you and daily check your e-mail messages for you. This way you will have an e-mail address that will make it far easier for employers to contact you using e-mail. It's worth a try.

2 Objective

The heading for the Objective section of the resume, as with other major resume section headings, should be centered on the page. It should also use the larger font size (12-point), should be set in all capital letters, and should be highlighted using bold type as shown on the resume sample.

When reviewing your resume, employers will immediately want to know what type of job you are seeking. This is why it is important for you to indicate this in the Objective section of the resume. In our sample resume, for example, William Davis has indicated he is seeking a position as a Line Mechanic—Manufacturing and Packaging.

If you don't spell out your job objective, the employer is left to guess what it is. Absence of an objective statement causes the employer to take an unneeded and unwanted extra step. You are forcing the company recruiter to contact you to determine if a specific job opening he or she has is of interest to you. If you are not interested, they have wasted their time. Most recruiters will simply move on to the next resume, when it is unclear what job the job seeker is looking for.

Review of the Objective section of several of the sample resumes contained in this book will show that, in most cases, they are straight-forward and fairly simple. Usually a job tile such as "Forklift Operator," "Machine Operator," or "Administrative Assistant" is all that is needed, unless you want to further qualify your requirements. The objective "Forklift Operator—Pharmaceutical Company," for example, gets pretty specific. It suggests that you would not work for a company unless they were in the pharmaceutical industry, which may not be the case at all.

In the example just cited, you might consider working as a Forklift Operator in a paper company, or a food company, or in a chemical manufacturing plant. If this is the case, you would want to exclude the words "Pharmaceutical Company" from your job objective. Otherwise, paper, food, or chemical companies may decide you are not interested in working for them, and would reject your resume right from the get-go. Choose your words carefully. Say what you mean, and mean what you say. It will make a difference on whether employers decide to screen you in or screen you out.

If you have more than one type or level of position in mind, list both positions in the job objective statement. Here are some examples:

- Executive Assistant/Administrative Assistant.
- Lead Operator or Machine Operator.
- Shipping Clerk/Forklift Operator/Warehouse Worker.
- Chemical Technician—Research or Process Control.

When you have one or more job objectives, always state your preferred objective first, followed by your second choice. Review of the sample resumes in this book will show you other examples of how to handle the situation when you have dual or multiple job objectives.

Never include two very different job objectives on the same resume. For example, if you were interested in a being a Veterinarian's Assistant or a Machine Operator, you would definitely not want to show this on the same resume. If you did and you were applying for a job as a Machine Operator, the employer might decide to pass on you since you might just quit and take a job as a Veterinarian's Assistant if such a job became available. In such cases, use two separate resumes, one showing your objective as Veterinarian's Assistant and the other resume listing your job objective as Machine Operator.

3 Summary

The Summary heading, as with other resume section headings, should be centered on the resume, use slightly larger (12-point) type, use all capital letters, and be highlighted using bold type. This helps to not only introduce this section of the resume but also to visually distinguish it from other resume sections.

The Summary section of the resume has a number of purposes, most of which are intended to stimulate the employer's interest in interviewing and hiring you. This is thought by many to be a very important element of the resume, so it needs to be done particularly well.

Before reading further, it is probably a good idea for you to read the Summary statement contained in this chapter's sample resume. By carefully studying the way this sample Summary statement is written, the directions that follow will make considerably more sense.

If you were an employer who wanted to hire a production worker, what are some of the characteristics you would be looking for in an employment candidate? Wouldn't you be seeking someone who is skilled, highly motivated, efficient, and productive—someone who is a self-starter, responsive, and quality-oriented? Of course you would. Now, if you were going to hire an accounting clerk or lab technician, wouldn't you also want to find someone who is skilled, thorough, accurate, analytical, efficient, and so on? Absolutely!

All of these adjectives are what we call favorable attributes or *positive personal descriptors*. Look at some of the sample resumes throughout this book and you will see how different job seekers have used these positive personal descriptors to describe themselves in the Summary statements of their resumes. For example, using the sample resume contained in this chapter, you will note that William Davis describes himself in very positive terms that an employer would find very desirable. Here are some of the adjectives and phrases he uses to make himself sound like a very attractive candidate:

- Skilled.
- Efficient.
- Hard-working.
- Motivated.
- Self-starter.
- Learns quickly.
- Operates effectively in a team environment (a team player).
- Strong technical contributor.
- Good communications and interpersonal skills.

Because Davis uses these positive personal descriptors to describe himself, it is impossible to read his resume Summary statement without having a very favorable impression of him. If, instead of using these descriptors, he would have used the Summary to simply say, "Line Mechanic with 10 years manufacturing experience," I'm sure you would agree that, as an employer, you would not find Davis to be quite as attractive a candidate. Keeping this in mind, now read the Summary statements of a number of the sample resumes. You will see many examples of how different job seekers used the Summary statement to make themselves sound like very desirable candidates. Using these positive descriptors wisely can definitely set you apart from other candidates and make you stand out in the eyes of an employer.

On pages 40–41 you will find a list of over 100 positive personal descriptors and introductory statements from which you can select. When selecting them, think about those attributes an employer would most likely think important to success in the job. Stated differently, what attributes would an employer want most to see in someone who is applying for the type of job you are seeking? Now find resume samples, later in this book, that most closely resemble the kind of job you want and see how these positive descriptors were used in the job seeker's Summary statement. You should be able to use one or more of these Summary statements as a guide for writing your own.

You will also note how various job seekers used these resume Summary sections to provide a brief description of their overall work experience as well. In this chapter's sample resume, for example, Davis summarizes his overall experience with the words "production mechanic with extensive experience in the

Positive Personal Descriptors
(Words you can use to describe yourself)

Positive Work Attributes:

Energetic	Conscientious	Focused	Goal-Oriented
High-Energy	Reliable	Committed	Quality-Focused
Dependable	Contributor	Willing	Self-Motivated
Motivated	Highly-Skilled	Thorough	Accurate
Skilled	Innovative	Dependable	Highly Dependable
Creative	Productive	Effective	Highly Productive
Efficient	Quick Learner	Learns Quickly	Quick Study
Self-Starter	Responsive	Decisive	Multi-Skilled
Knowledgeable	Practical	Spirited	Well-Trained
Hands-On	Methodical	Quality-Oriented	Customer-Focused
Analytical	Seasoned	Experienced	Industrious
Organized	Attentive	Careful	Detail-Oriented
Solid Producer	Proficient	Bright	Articulate
Responsive	Confident	Intelligent	Improvement-Oriented
Prompt	Positive	Determined	
Resilient	Courageous	Disciplined	Loyal/Dedicated
Trustworthy	Dedicated	Action-Oriented	Logical
Hardworking			

Strong Work Ethic (fill in the blanks):

Key contributor to _____

Noted for _____

Solid _____ skills

Skilled in the use of _____

Talented _____

Solid reputation for _____

Strong reputation for _____

Extensive experience in _____

Played key role in _____

Strong reputation as _____

Skilled at _____

Positive Personal Descriptors *(Continued)*

Trained in _____

Well trained and skilled in _____

Demonstrated leadership in _____

Strong reputation for _____

Enjoy working with (or at) _____

Social Skills:

Friendly	Outgoing	Charismatic	Team-Focused
Team Player	Team-Oriented	Open	Flexible
Adaptive	Personable	Pleasant	Courteous
Sensitive	Supportive	Good Listener	Sensitive
Diplomatic	Respectful		

Good oral communication skills

Excellent oral communication skills

Good written communication skills

Excellent written communication skills

Good oral and written communication skills

Excellent oral and written communication skills

Strong interpersonal skills

Excellent interpersonal skills

Solid team player

---

installation and start-up of new packaging line equipment, including operator training, safety, reliability, and ergonomics." This is a pretty good general statement that does an excellent job of briefly describing his overall job experience and skill level.

Here are some other examples of similar statements that different workers have used to describe their work experience or primary skill area in the resume Summary section.

"Skilled electrician with over 15 years of experience in the installation, start-up, troubleshooting, repair and maintenance of electric power and power distribution systems in a manufacturing environment."

"Skilled Machine Operator with 17 years experience in the operation of a 3,000 feet-per-minute, high-speed paper machine (80 tons per day)."

"Talented, industrious Legal Assistant with over 10 years experience in general practice and criminal law."

"Skilled, seasoned Floor Installer with over 8 years experience in the installation of a wide range of tile, vinyl, and hard-wood flooring."

To have maximum positive effect, the Summary section of your resume needs to provide a brief but broad description of your overall work experience and should make use of "positive descriptors" to set you apart from other job seekers and stimulate an employer's interest in hiring you. Where possible, it should also serve to highlight some of your most salable skills and talents. Careful review of the resume samples contained in this book should prove enormously helpful to you in creating a very effective Summary section.

While the information from this section is fresh in your mind, try writing your Summary statement. Don't be surprised if it takes several rewrites until you get something that sounds pretty good. Using the resume samples provided in this book as a guide for modeling your Summary statement should make the job much easier. Therefore, I recommend you find a resume sample that resembles the type job you are looking for, and use the Summary statement contained in that resume as a starting point. This will save you a lot of time and work.

EXPERIENCE

The Experience section of the resume (sample resume section numbers 4, 5, and 6) is designed to describe, in some detail, your specific work experience. It has three components:

1. Company name and description (see sample resume section ④).
2. Job title and description (see sample resume section ⑤).
3. Job duties and accomplishments (see sample resume section ⑥).

Before we describe each of these resume components, take a minute or two to take a look at the general design and layout of this section of the resume. Note the effective use of white space to create visual separation between these three resume elements. This makes the resume more visually pleasing and easier to read then if these sections were crammed together. Additionally, you will notice the use of bold print to highlight the company name, employment dates, and job title. This provides good visual separation between the three resume components, making the resume easy to read, and making it easier for an employer to distinguish between company name and description (the "company section") and job title and description (the "job section"). This visual separation is further enhanced by spelling out the company name in all capital letters, while the job title uses a combination of both capital letters and small letters.

Employment dates—those dates during which you have worked for the company—are also in bold type, but are set at the extreme right margin of the page. Putting these dates in this position allows you much more space for writing your job description and your job duties and accomplishments.

Although the sample resume in this chapter doesn't show this, if you held more than one job for the same employer, you would include the job dates for each job immediately next to the job title in brackets. For example:

1. **Administrative Assistant** (2003 to Present)
   File Clerk (2001 to 2003)
2. **Packaging Machine Operator** (2002 to 2005)
   Warehouse Worker (1998 to 2002)

Also, when using dates, either employment dates or job dates, use years only. Do not show months or days. You will notice this in the examples just shown, as well as the sample resumes throughout this book. If an employer needs to know specific dates, they will ask you for this information during the job interview or on the employment application that they may ask you to fill out.

Finally, as on the sample resume contained in this chapter, you will notice that bullet points are used to set job duties and accomplishments (see resume section ⑥) apart from the job title and brief job description (see resume section ⑤) shown immediately above. This again creates good visual separation between these two distinct but important resume components, making it easier for the employer to quickly distinguish between the two. Additionally, highlighting job duties and accomplishments by using bullets will highlight your specific experience, skills, and accomplishments—all qualifications that employers are going to be most interested in learning more about during the job interview.

We will now break out and discuss all three components of the Experience section of the resume, so that you will know exactly how to prepare and write these sections.

④ Company Name and Description

Take a moment or two to look at the company name and description section of the sample resume contained in this chapter. Than read a couple more company description sections in some of the other sample resumes later in this book. Doing so will give you a general feel for how to write these descriptions and what they typically contain. It will also make the following discussion much easier to follow.

First, you will notice that the company name is set in bold type and uses all capital letters. As mentioned earlier, this makes it easier for the employer to visually distinguish between the company section and the job section of the resume. For example, if the employer is looking to see if you have had experience with a specific company, it makes it easier to see this. It also serves to highlight the company's name, which can be helpful if you have worked for a well-known or highly respected company. The location at which you worked is then set in normal type and positioned directly next to the company name. The location also uses a combination of capital and small letters, as shown on the resume sample.

You will also note the placement of employment dates (the dates you have worked for the company) in bold type at the right margin and on the same line as the company name. This helps the employer recognize that these are employment dates rather than job dates. Job dates, as you will recall, are placed in brackets directly next to their corresponding job title.

In the example, William Davis held only one job with Mason Products, Inc. This is also true with Packo Equipment Company. In these cases, the employment date and job date are the same. If they are identical, as in the Davis resume example, you only need to show employment dates. There is no need to also show job dates in brackets next to each job title. Job dates are evident from the employment dates shown at the right margin of the resume. If Davis had held more than one job with Mason or Packo, he would include job dates, in brackets, next to each job title as well.

The company title is then followed by a one or two sentence description of the company and/or plant facility in which you worked. Such company descriptions normally include the following elements:

- Type of company (manufacturing, insurance company, law firm, etc.).
- Company or plant size (sales volume, number of employees, etc.).
- Products manufactured or services/goods sold.

Here are some examples of company descriptions:

"A 350-employee paper manufacturing plant producing sanitary tissue products (facial tissue, toilet tissue, napkins, and towels) sold through paper distributors to retail outlets."

"A leading, $5 billion insurance company selling a full range of commercial and residential lines including general liability, auto, and structural loss coverages."

"A janitorial services company providing cleaning services to a wide range of retail stores and commercial office buildings in the Philadelphia region."

These examples, as well as those contained in the resume samples provided later in this book, should give you a good idea how to describe the companies you have worked for.

Employers are typically looking for employment candidates who have worked in similar industries and companies. Such candidates' working experiences are more closely related to the employer's own requirements and suggest that these candidates will require far less training than those without this background. Since employers may not be familiar with your company, it is always a good idea to include this brief company description so they can better assess your fit for the position they are attempting to fill. Not providing this information on your resume could place you at a serious competitive disadvantage, compared to those candidates who do, and the employer may thus move right on to the next candidate's resume.

Rather than reading further, I recommend you take a breather and, while the information is fresh in your mind, try writing company descriptions for each of the companies for whom you have worked. To make the job easier, use the sample resumes provided later in the book to try and find a company or plant that sounds similar to your own employer(s). Although this may take a little time to do, if you find one, it could save you a great deal of time and make the job easier.

⑤ Job Title and Description

As previously discussed, this section of the resume begins with the job title. The job title should be in bold type and is written using a combination of capital (upper-case) and small (lower-case) letters. Also, as stated earlier, if you have held more than one job with a given employer, you will want to include the job dates directly to the right of the job title and enclosed these dates in brackets. However, as you will recall, job dates are not needed if you have only held one job with the employer.

It is recommended that you start preparing to write this section, by studying the job title and description section (section ⑤) of the sample resume contained in this chapter. Then also review the same section of a few more of the sample resumes contained in the next chapter of this book. You will note that these uniformly contain the following two basic elements or components:

1. Reporting relationship.
2. Broad statement of overall job responsibility.

Here are a couple more examples:

- *Forklift Operator*
  "Report to Warehouse Supervisor with responsibility for operating a forklift truck in the timely delivery of raw materials and packaging supplies to 6 paper manufacturing and finishing lines."
- *Senior Administrative Assistant*
  "Report to the Corporate Controller with responsibility for providing a full range of secretarial and administrative support services to the Controller and his staff of 4 key managers."
- *Electronics Repair Technician*
  "Report to the Electrical Maintenance Supervisor with responsibility for installation, testing, troubleshooting, and repair of manufacturing instrumentation and control systems in a polyethylene manufacturing plant."

As you can see from reviewing these and other examples from this book, the job description statement begins with reporting relations. Simply stating "report to" (or "reported to," if it is a past job) followed by your boss' job title is all that is needed to describe your reporting relationship.

You will immediately want to follow the description of reporting relationship with a broad description of your overall job responsibility. This is easily accomplished by stating "with responsibility for," and than list the basic services or functions for which you were accountable. Keep the job description fairly broad and general, describing your overall responsibility, not your individual job duties. Specific duties are included in the next section of the resume (see section ⑥ of the sample resume).

Whenever possible, it is a good idea to provide some quantitative dimensions that convey the size and/or complexity of your job. In the previous examples, for instance, the Forklift Operator provided delivery to **6** paper manufacturing and finishing lines. Use of the number "6" is more impressive and suggests a more responsible, demanding job than if we had simply stated that the Forklift Operator provided delivery to paper manufacturing and finishing lines. Likewise, in the Administrative Assistant job description, stating that in addition to serving the Controller, the Assistant also provided support services to **4** additional staff managers, suggests a more responsible and demanding job than if we didn't bother to mention the number of staff managers. As you can see, adding some quantitative dimensions to your job description can provide a whole new meaning to the size and/or importance of your job.

As with other sections of the resume, previously described, it is a good idea to see if you can locate a resume from among the many resume samples that closely approximates the type of job you are seeking. Even more specifically, see if you can find a resume or resumes that contain job descriptions similar to the kinds of jobs you have held or currently hold. Review of the job descriptions from these resumes should give you a good jumpstart in writing such descriptions for your own resume.

Before proceeding to the next section of your resume, it is suggested you take time out to prepare a company title and descriptions for each of your current and past employers. Do this while the learning is still fresh in your mind, and then take a break before moving on to the next resume section. Remember, you want to be eating this elephant one bite at a time. It's a big elephant and you don't want to get too full before you take the next bite.

⑥ Job Duties and Accomplishments

The next section of the resume (see section ⑥ of the sample resume) begins a bulleted listing of your job duties and accomplishments. You will notice how the use of bullets sets this section apart from other resume sections, making it stand out. This is important because it focuses the employer on the specifics of your job duties, calling attention to not only these duties but also your relevant skills and accomplishments. How well this section is written can have a huge impact on the employer and, if well written, will differentiate you from other job candidates and motivate the employer to schedule you for a job interview.

You will want to write this section of the resume with two objectives in mind. First, you will want to provide a fairly comprehensive listing of your job duties so that the employer has a solid understanding of your overall job responsibilities. Second, where possible, you will want to cite specific job accomplishments or results achieved that suggest you are a dedicated and productive employee. The later is particularly important if you want to really stand out and encourage employers to interview you.

Describing Job Duties

Before getting into detailed instructions on describing your job duties, it is important to provide you with some basic writing tricks and techniques that will help you to write more powerful and effective resume statements. When describing job duties, start each statement with a verb, and then follow it with the specific job duty or responsibility. Here are a few examples, so you can see what I am talking about:

Example 1: Job Duties   Shift Mechanic—Paper Finishing

- Provides quick diagnosis and rapid mechanical repair of high-speed paper finishing equipment to ensure minimum line downtown and product waste.
- Maintains complete, accurate repair records as the basis for predictive and preventive maintenance planning.
- Fine-tune sensitive electromechanical adjustments involving split-second timing and close tolerance settings.
- Performs daily shift inspections of all equipment to spot and anticipate mechanical failures before they occur.
- Carries out maintenance in accordance with preventive maintenance program schedule.
- Ensures that Stores maintains proper inventories of critical machine parts to avoid delays and unscheduled line downtime.

Example 2: Job Duties   Administrative Assistant—Procurement

- Provides secretarial and administrative support to Corporate Procurement Manager and 3 Purchasing Agents.
- Answers, screens, and routes phone calls to Procurement Staff.
- Reads, screens, and routes department mail, directly responding to routine inquiries.
- Reads, screens, and prioritizes Manager's e-mails.
- Schedules and coordinates meetings with Staff, internal clients, and vendors.
- Types purchase orders, purchase order releases, contracts, and general correspondence in support of Procurement function.
- Assists in the preparation, mailing, collection, and evaluation of requests-for-proposals and contract bids from vendors.

- Maintains all vendor and contract files.
- Assists Accounts Payable in reconciling vendor invoice issues with purchase orders and contract requirements.
- Prepares PowerPoint presentations and handouts to support large group meetings and presentations to senior management.

Example 3: Job Duties   Forklift Operator—Vital Supplies Delivery

- Drives forklift truck in the delivery of palletized packaging materials and vital supplies to Finishing Department production units.
- Continually inventories production units' on-floor inventory supply levels of tail glue, paper cores, poly wrap, and corrugated knockdown cartons to determine and anticipate delivery needs.
- Juggles delivery schedule to ensure timely delivery of supplies, avoiding shutdowns and costly machine downtime.
- Uses wireless electronic transmitter to track and record inventory withdrawals and deliveries.
- Inputs delivery time, finishing unit number, product name, code, volume and control numbers, thereby maintaining accurate and up-to-date warehouse inventory count.
- Performs end-of-shift physical inventory count of remaining vital supplies and reconciles count with beginning-of-shift inventory levels and on-shift deliveries.
- Ensures that warehouse inventories of vital supplies remain at planned levels to avoid out-of-stock emergencies resulting in machine downtime.
- Returns out-of-specification materials from finishing unit to warehouse "reclaim area" for return shipment to vendor.
- Ensures the safe and careful operation of forklift vehicle at all times.

You can see from these examples that by starting each job duty statement with a verb you are forced to be brief and concise. Notice how concise these sample statements are.

If you have difficulty defining your job duties, try answering the following questions:

1. Why does my job exist?
2. What does the organization get (or what is created) from the work I do?
3. What are the key things I must do to accomplish my job?
4. What are the steps I take when performing my job?
5. When I track my daily routine from the beginning of my workday until I leave, what are the functions I carry out and the tasks I perform?

By systematically tracking each of the tasks you perform during the course of the workday and why you perform them, you should be able to readily define each of your key job duties. If you still have trouble, however, see if you can find a similar job from among the many sample resumes in this book and see how the principal job duties for this position are described.

Job Duties versus Accomplishments

Most resumes are little more than a job description, listing the key duties and responsibilities of the job. Although this is certainly quite acceptable and provides important information that employers need in order to judge your qualifications, resumes can be much more powerful when they also include some key or unique accomplishments—specific things the candidate did (other than perform their usual duties) to bring about improvement. These could include special things that increased efficiency, reduced costs, saved time, improved quality, provided a safer work environment, or in some other way had a positive impact on the organization. It could be something you did on your own or as a part of a team.

Drawing from this book's sample resumes, here are a few concrete examples of what I mean:

- "Served as a key member of start-up team, responsible for the successful installation, start-up, and debugging of a $5 MM household cleaners packaging line."

- "Reduced unscheduled downtime from 1 hour to 15 minutes per shift through use of predictive maintenance approach."

- "Consistently met or exceeded line production and quality goals."

- "Served on Plant Safety Committee that reduced lost-time injuries by 50 percent in a single year through implementation of safety awareness training program."

- "Suggested a change in repack work procedure that resulted in 10 percent gain in Repack Department productivity."

- "Participated as a member of Plant Cost Reduction Taskforce that identified over $¼ MM in annual waste reduction cost saving."

Put yourself in the employer's shoes for a moment. If you were looking at the resumes of a number of candidates with similar work experience, but one candidate had two or more of the above accomplishments, wouldn't you have a preference for this candidate? Of course you would. Employers are always looking for above-average employees—those who are efficient and productive—those who have a history of improving things and adding value to the organization. When it comes to employment, hiring managers and supervisors are always looking for that one candidate who will go the extra mile.

Here are some questions that might help jog your memory about special contributions you made, either by yourself or as part of a team.

1. Were you a member of a start-up team that successfully started up new equipment or a new manufacturing line?

2. Did you or your work team meet or exceed any production or quality goals?

3. Did you make an suggestions or recommendations that led to:

   a. Time savings?

   b. Increased productivity?

   c. Cost savings?

   d. Quality improvement?

   e. Reduced waste?

   f. Safer work environment?

   g. Reduced injuries?

   h. Other kinds of improvement?

4. Did you ever work as part of a team or committee whose work brought about:

   a. Times savings?

   b. Increased productivity?

   c. Cost savings?

   d. Quality improvement?

   e. Reduced waste?

   f. Safer work environment?

   g. Reduces injuries?

   h. Other kinds of improvement?

If you can answer "yes" to any of these questions, you have an excellent opportunity to add some key accomplishment statements to your resume. Take full advantage of this opportunity; it will help you stand out from the masses. Although not all of this book's sample resumes include such accomplishment statements, I would strongly recommend you look through the sample resumes to spot some that do. They will give you some good ideas on how to word these accomplishment statements. The sample resume contained in this chapter is a good place to start.

You will notice, as with statements describing your job duties, accomplishment statements also start with a verb. Additionally, in many cases, these statements also show a specific, measurable result.

That is, they indicate the amount of cost savings, percent improvement, specific production volume increase amounts, and so on. These are concrete measurements that convey the degree of improvement brought about by the job seeker's efforts (either individually or as part of a team).

Before moving on to the next section of the resume and while the information for this resume component is still fresh in your mind, it is strongly recommended that you stop at this point and take time to systematically develop the Job Duties and Accomplishments section for both your current and past positions. This is perhaps the biggest part of the elephant, and you'll want to bite off one piece at a time so that you avoid getting a major case of indigestion. It is also very important to the effectiveness and impact of your resume that you take your time and do a really good job of developing this important resume segment.

Resume Length

You want to remember that you will need to keep your total resume to no more than two pages in length. Obviously, therefore, it will not be necessary to develop a full-blown job description and listing of job duties and accomplishments for *all* past jobs you have held during the course of your entire career. In most cases, there will not be enough room on the resume to spell out the details of these earlier positions.

The reality is that employers are most interested in your current job and the jobs that you have held most recently in your career. They have little or no interest, for example, in positions you held 15 or 20 years ago. So, you will not want to commit much resume space to these earlier jobs. In the interests of conserving resume space, therefore you will want to show only job title and job dates for these earlier jobs. There is no need to include a job description or listing of key duties and accomplishments. This will save you considerable time and effort, allowing you to focus on developing detailed information only on your last job or two.

7 Education

The Education section of the resume (see sample resume section 7) shows your formal educational training such as high school, trade school, or college level education that you have received. This is different from the "Company Training" section of the resume, which highlights basic training courses or seminars provided as part of a company's internally sponsored employee development programs. Typically, these company training sessions are no more than a day or two in duration, whereas formal education normally is offered by an educational institution outside of the company and results in the student being awarded a formal degree or diploma.

As with other resume section headings, the Education heading is in bold type, uses larger (12-point) type size, and is centered on the resume page. Note the extra white space separating this heading from the list of job duties and accomplishments shown in the previous section of the resume. This provides the proper visual separation between these two resume sections, making it easier for the employer to read the resume.

When listing your educational qualifications, always show your highest level of education first. For example, if you hold an associates degree and also have a high school diploma, you will want to first list your associates degree, followed by your high school credentials. If you completed high school and then went on to complete a formal program at a trade or technical school, which resulted in your being awarded a diploma, you will then want to show this advanced education first, followed by your high school credentials.

In displaying educational credentials, always start with the degree or diploma awarded, followed by the name of the school and graduation date on the next line. As shown on the sample resume, for example, Davis first shows "High School Diploma," which is followed on the next line by the school's name (Utica High School) and date of graduation (1995), separated by a comma.

If you were awarded an associates degree, you will also want to show your major area of study. This is especially true if your major is directly or closely related to the type of position you are seeking. Thus, if you were applying for a job as a Junior Accountant, and you received an associates degree in accounting, this would be shown on the resume as follows:

AA Degree, Accounting
Weidner University, 2002

If you had undertaken a formal educational program, but had not yet completed the full program before seeking employment, you could show this on the resume in one of two ways as follow:

Example 1:   AA Degree Program
Major: Accounting
Weidner University, 2001–2002
(25 Credit Hours Complete)

Example 2:   AA Degree Program (12 Credits)
Major: Accounting
Weidner University, 2001–2002
Courses: Fundamentals of Accounting
   Accounting Software
   Tax Accounting 101
   Reading Financial Statements
   Business Law

In both cases, it is clear to the employer that you have not yet graduated, but are either currently enrolled or have completed specific coursework. You will note in the sample resume provided in this chapter, Davis has not yet completed the full program at Albany Technical Institute, so he has chosen to list the relevant courses he has taken in the Education section.

Where to Position the Education Section on the Resume

Although with heavily experienced job seekers Education is usually positioned on page two of the resume, there are some occasions when it might be advantageous to position it on the first page instead. When this option is chosen, the Education section is placed immediately following the Summary section, but before the Experience section.

Here are some basic guidelines for determining whether you should show Education on page 1 or page 2 of your resume:

1. If your education is relatively recent (within the last three years) and is related to the type of work you are seeking, put it on page 1 of the resume.

2. If your education is ancient history (completed more than three years ago), or if it is not directly related to the type of work you are seeking, place it on page 2 of your resume.

3. If your education is from a very prestigious or highly regarded school in your occupational specialty, then list it on page 1 of your resume. (For example, if you received a diploma from a well-known trade school as a Machinist, and you are looking for a job as a Machinist, having education on page 1 of your resume, rather than page 2, would definitely be to your advantage.)

8 Company Training

The next section of the resume, company training (see section 8 of the sample resume) follows Education and lists the various company-sponsored training programs you have completed. Do not overdo this section of the resume by listing every single seminar or training program you have ever taken over the past 30 years of your employment. List only those programs that you have completed in the past 10 years or so, and that are related to the type of position you are seeking.

For example, if you are looking for a job as an Accounting Clerk, and you completed a course in hairdressing last year, you do not want to show this on your resume. Doing so might cause an employer to question the sincerity of your interest in an Accounting Clerk's position. It may suggest to the employer that if the right hairdressing job were to come along you might decide to leave for this other position, wasting the employer's time and requiring them to take additional time to train a replacement. Or, if you are applying for a job as a production worker in a factory, the fact that you took a first aid course 20 years ago is not going to be of much interest to an employer. So, keep training programs listed in this section to those that were completed within the past 10 years or less, and that are related to the type of work you are seeking.

When listing company-provided training courses and seminars on your resume, list only the title or name of the training program. There is no need to list dates or provide a course description. The title alone will provide the employer with all the information he or she needs to know. If the employer wants more information than that, he or she will ask for this during the job interview.

When listing courses or seminars, you will first want to list those that are most related to the type of work you are looking for. So, if you were a Mechanic, for example, you would first want to list various mechanical or machine repair courses you have completed. Courses in forklift truck operation and safety, for example, would then be listed after the mechanical related coursework, since these, although important, are not nearly as important as the mechanical courses you have completed.

9 **Computer Skills**

Unless you are applying for a job where you are absolutely certain that computer skills will not be required, you will want to use the next section of the resume to highlight your computer skills. Today, increasingly, more and more jobs are requiring computer skills of some sort. In fact, the numbers of jobs not requiring these skills seem to be fewer and fewer each year. The computer seems to be touching almost every facet of our lives whether you are an Accounting Clerk, Administrative Assistant, Laboratory Technician, Waitress, Warehouse Worker or a manufacturing Production Worker.

As with all prior resume sections, the Computer Skills section heading is set in bold type, uses larger (12-point) type size, and is typed using all capital letters. You will again notice, when viewing the Davis sample resume, how adequate white space is used to visually separate this resume section from the previous section of the resume.

In the case of administrative support jobs, such as Clerks or Administrative Assistants, it will probably be sufficient to simply list the various software with which are familiar. For example, a simple listing of computer software skills might look as follows:

Computer Skills:

> MS Word
>
> Excel
>
> PowerPoint
>
> MS Outlook
>
> ACT
>
> QuickBooks Pro

As a Production Worker, you may not be working with personal computers but, instead, could easily be working with manufacturing control systems. If so, you will want to list them. The Davis sample resume contained in this chapter, for instance, shows that Davis is experienced with Honeywell TDC 3000 control systems. Others, like Warehouse Workers or employees working in the Stores area, might be working with administrative control systems such as SAP, or as a Laboratory Technician you might be working with statistical software such as SAS. Whether an expert or simply a user of these systems, you will want to highlight these computer skills in the Computer Skills section of your resume.

For those working in technology-related jobs where both hardware and software knowledge are routinely required, you will want to show both on your resume. In this case, you may want to separate the Computer Skills area of the resume into two categories, hardware and software. For instance:

Hardware	*Software*
Personal Computers	MS Access
Laptops	SAP
Mini Computers	SAS
Microprocessors	HTML
LANS	JAVA
WANS	Excel

LICENSES AND CERTIFICATIONS

Although not shown on the Davis sample resume in this chapter, this section might be included on the resume. This is particularly true of those seeking jobs in occupations that require licensing such as Nurses and Electricians. If you possess a license you will want to show that in this section of the resume.

The data shown normally includes name of the license, license number, issuing authority, and date of issuance. For example:

Registered Practical Nurse
Commonwealth of Pennsylvania, 2004
License #: PA-0037-792

A WORD ABOUT AGE DISCRIMINATION

Although things have improved somewhat in recent years due to the gradual aging of the U.S. workforce, you need to be aware that age discrimination is still alive and well in America. As disappointing as this may sound to older workers, it is unfortunately a reality and you need to be sensitive to this fact when preparing your resume.

According to the U.S. government, the issue of age discrimination typically begins to set in after age 40. This means that workers over age 40 are protected against age discrimination under federal laws, and can file lawsuits where they feel employers have used age to discriminate against them.

What can you do to protect yourself against this age discrimination possibility?

If age is a potential issue, you may want to consider dropping some of your earlier jobs off the resume entirely. If later, during a job interview, you are asked why you did this, simply explain that due to limited resume space you felt it was more important to use this space to cite your current qualifications rather than waste it describing earlier jobs that have little or no bearing on the kind of job you are seeking. In almost all cases, the employer will be satisfied and move on with the rest of the interview.

If the employer continues to question why you dropped these jobs from the resume, then simply say that you were also concerned about the possibility of age discrimination. At this point, you can expect that the employer will drop this subject like a hot potato and continue on with the job interview.

5

Sample Resumes

BARBARA N. SNEIDER
21 Harborview Terrace, 2-C
Dana Pointe, CA 23859
Email: BarSnei21@AOL.com

Home: (402) 663-0978

Office: (949) 757-9263

OBJECTIVE

Executive Administrative Assistant

SUMMARY

Seasoned Executive Administrative Assistant with excellent organization and administrative skills. Highly efficient, motivated executive assistant experienced at handling huge work volume, juggling priorities, and performing well in a demanding, high-pressure work environment. Noted for strong interpersonal and communication skills.

EXPERIENCE

BAKER CHEMICAL COMPANY, INC., Ocean Park, CA   **2003 to Present**
A $ 3.2 billion international manufacturer and distributor of specialty and commodity chemicals with operations in 36 countries.

Executive Administrative Assistant
Provide a broad range of administrative support services to the Corporate Secretary and the Associate General Counsel, International.

- Composes, types and proofreads letters, legal documents, charts, and tables.
- Prepares PowerPoint slides and presentations with appropriate handouts and graphics.
- Screens all incoming phone calls, fielding many routine requests and conserving executive's time.
- Plans in-house and offsite meetings and conferences including facility layout, equipment needs, transportation, meals, lodging, and recreational activities for attendees.
- Opens, screens, prioritizes, and routes incoming mail and other correspondence.
- Maintains and updates an impeccable filing system.
- Maintains calendars, schedules meetings, and appointments.
- Arranges domestic and international travel schedules and itineraries.
- Prepares general and travel expense vouchers.
- Verifies and processes outside counsel invoices

BAXTER TECHNOLOGIES, LLC, Carlsbad, CA   **1999 – 2003**
High-growth technology company engaged in providing e-business solutions in the handling of secured financial transactions via the Internet.

Executive Administrative Assistant
Provided administrative support to the Directors of eBusiness Strategy & Technology and Converged IP Solutions and 7 other managers. Worked in a dynamic, high-pressure executive environment.

- Managed frequent, complex domestic and international travel arrangements.
- Handled challenging calendar and meeting scheduling demands.
- Coordinated international and domestic meetings, including meeting logistics and setup.
- Prepared and processed expense reports, time reports, and purchase requisitions.
- Provided typing, phone answering, and general administrative support.

Barbara N. Sneider   **Page 2**

SECURITY FORCE, INC., San Diego, CA   **1996 – 1999**
Contract security company providing security guard services to manufacturing and retail operations
throughout the southwestern U.S. and West Coast.

Administrative Assistant
Reported to the Director of Sales – Western Region.

- Prepared contracts for security services.
- Kept accurate records, files and reports for sales and accounting purposes.
- Processed paperwork for new account sales.
- Made travel arrangements, scheduled appointments and meetings.
- Provided full range of administrative support services including phone answering, mail screening, typing, preparation of PowerPoint presentations, etc.

PACIFIC BELL, Los Angeles, CA   **1992 - 1996**
Customer Consultant
Reported to the Manager of Customer Service with responsibility for fielding customer complaints and
inquiries.

- Handled demanding customer complaints.
- Coordinated troubleshooting of customer billing and service problems.
- Ensured customers were happy and satisfied with services provided.

EDUCATION

High School Diploma
Irving High School, 1992

ADMINISTRATIVE & COMPUTER SKILLS

Type 110 Words-Per-Minute (With High Accuracy)
Microsoft PowerPoint
Microsoft Word
Microsoft Excel
Microsoft Project
QuickBooks Pro
Outlook Express
ACT for Windows

JANET A. ANDERSON

825 Michaelson Way
Plano, TX 12348
Phone: (602) 495-3249
Email: JANA825@AOL.com

OBJECTIVE

Administrative Assistant

SUMMARY

Talented, motivated Administrative Assistant with strong administrative support skills. Over 9 years experience in health-care environment. Solid computer skills; fast, accurate typist; excellent telephone and interpersonal skills; skilled communicator (verbal and written); exceptional organizational and work management skills. Works efficiently in a fast-paced, high-volume, demanding work environment.

EXPERIENCE

NEWSTAR HEALTH SYSTEMS, Plano, TX   **2001 to Present**
Eight-hundred bed hospital and health-care complex serving Plano, Texas and surrounding area.

Administrative Assistant
Reported to Chief Administrator with responsibility for providing broad range of administrative support services in support of hospital and related health-care operations.

- Composes and draft letters, memos, and reports for review and approval.
- Assists in resolving highly aged accounts receivable.
- Acts as liaison between Chief Administrator and Billing staff.
- Plans and schedules meetings; maintains calendars.
- Interacts with auxiliary departments, management, and clients maintaining solid relationships and good rapport.
- Effectively balances competing priorities and tight deadlines.
- Prepares a variety of presentations and reports using MS PowerPoint and Excel.
- Trains new employees on billing procedures.

DOCTOR BILLING SERVICES, INC., Dallas, TX   **1996 – 2001**
Outside service bureau contractor providing billing and collection services for health-care providers, both hospitals and physician practices.

Administrative Assistant
Reported to President with accountability for providing full range of administrative support services.

- Drafted and typed a wide range of letters, memos, and reports.
- Answered phones and effectively handled high volume of incoming calls.
- Managed daily calendar, coordinating appointments, and scheduling meetings.
- Used advanced features of MS Word and PowerPoint to prepare high-impact presentations.
- Maintained computerized account database, generating key status reports.
- Developed and maintained an organized filing system.

- Handled travel arrangements and planned major company events.
- Provided general direction to office staff with diverse duties.

EDUCATION

A.A. Degree – Administrative Services
Waverly Community College, 1996

High School Diploma
Plano High School, 1994

COMPUTER SKILLS

MS Word
MS Works
MS PowerPoint
MS Access
MS Outlook
MS Project
Various Windows Platforms

MARGUERITE E. HARRINGTON
2655 Apple Lane
Princeton, NJ 13427

Home: (609) 447-9326   Email: MarHar26@AOL.com   Office: (609) 574-2139

OBJECTIVE

Administrative Assistant / Office Manager

SUMMARY

CPS (Certified Professional Secretary) and CAM (Certified Administrative Manager) with over 15 years experience in the secretarial and administrative fields. Exceptional typing, organizational, PC, word-processing, stenographic, file maintenance, computational and bookkeeping skills. Solid communications and interpersonal skills. Highly personable with excellent professional image.

EXPERIENCE

WEBSTER FLEET LEASING, INC., Trenton, NJ   **2002 to Present**
Major automobile fleet leasing company providing fleet auto leasing and services to a wide range of U.S. companies.

Leasing Assistant
Report to National Manager of Leasing & Fleet Maintenance with responsibility for providing a broad range of secretarial and administrative support services.

- Maintain complex filing system for over 500 major auto fleet accounts.
- Create and maintain various information databases required for management of fleet accounts.
- Review and monitor fleet driver invoices for reimbursement of auto repairs.
- Research, evaluate and recommend various vendors for fleet equipment purchase, parts, repairs, etc., to secure best prices and lowest cost.
- Prepare and process purchase requisitions for purchase of fleet equipment and repairs.
- Investigate, review, approve and process fleet insurance claims submitted by drivers.
- Research and investigate motor vehicle history of fleet drivers.
- Type correspondence, memos, and letters; create posters, flyers, brochures, programs, etc.
- Perform other typical administrative support duties as needed.

FURLONG CONSULTING, LLC, Philadelphia, PA   **1996 - 2002**
Privately-held computer consulting firm involved in the design, installation and start-up of Intranet systems for client companies. Company has offices in Florida, Georgia and North Carolina.

Executive Assistant
Reported to CEO with accountability for providing a broad range of administrative support services in support of business operation.

- Processed new hires, including basic company orientation and benefit sign-up.
- Prepared consultant bios for use with marketing and sales literature.

Marguerite E. Harrington   **Page 2**

- Used QuickBooks Pro to input and process weekly payroll run.
- Processed consultant timesheets and expense reports.
- Prepared client billing and tracked invoices.
- Created and maintained Excel spreadsheets for company budget, check register, payroll, accounts payable and accounts receivable.
- Used QuickBooks Pro to generate various financial reports when requested.
- Prepared and processed various checks for signature and payment.
- Received and deposited monies into company bank account.
- Maintained petty cash fund, keeping accurate deposit and withdrawal records.
- Opened, screened and distributed incoming mail.
- Screened and directed incoming phone calls.
- Prepared and typed a wide range of correspondence, letters and reports.

UNIVERSITY OF DELAWARE, Newark, DE   **1989 – 1996**

Office Manager
Worked as Office Manager for various departments at the University of Delaware. Typical duties included:

- Composing and typing letters and other correspondence.
- Formulating, creating and typing forms.
- Creating and maintaining records.
- Screening and directing phone calls.
- Review and approval of employee timesheets.
- Researching and answering questions regarding paycheck discrepancies.
- Maintaining confidential personnel records.
- Interviewing and hiring of clerical personnel.
- Ordering and maintaining supply inventories.

EDUCATION / CERTIFICATIONS

Certified Administrative Manager
Canadian Institute of Management, 1989

Certified Professional Secretary
Institute for Secretarial Certification, 1987

Notary Public
State of Delaware, 1990

COMPUTER SKILLS

MS Office Suite (Excel, Word, PowerPoint)
QuickBooks Pro, MS Project, Access Database, ACT Database

KATHERINE T. MATTINGS
162 Marion Road
Princeton, NJ 13246

Home: (609) 552-0978   Email: KatMat@AOL.com   Office: (609) 552-8886

OBJECTIVE

Administrative Assistant - Operations / Manufacturing

SUMMARY

Bright, articulate, motivated Administrative Assistant who enjoys working in a fast-paced, high demand operations or manufacturing environment. Highly organized and efficient worker who performs well under pressure and can meet tight deadlines with high level of accuracy. Excellent secretarial, interpersonal and communication skills. Noted for ability to streamline processes and procedures, saving both time and money.

EXPERIENCE

WEATHERBY COPORATION, Trenton, NJ   **1995 to Present**
A $500 million, leading manufacturer of safety equipment including safety goggles, hard hats, protective gloves and clothing.

Administrative Assistant   (2000 to Present)
Reports to the corporate Manufacturing Manager, providing a complete range of secretarial and administrative duties in support of the Corporate Manufacturing function.

- Collects and summarizes daily manufacturing reports from three plant locations.
- Tracks and reports statistical data including daily production volume, volume shipped, waste and spoilage, employee accidents and lost-time injuries – by plant and overall.
- Schedules appointments and meeting for Manufacturing Manager using Microsoft Outlook.
- Answers and screens incoming telephone calls.
- Types a wide range of correspondence, summaries and manufacturing reports.
- Prepares PowerPoint presentations and handouts for meetings with plant manufacturing staffs and company senior management.
- Sorts and screens incoming mail.
- Sets up special manufacturing rewards and recognition programs, including site selection, dinner reservations, and the ordering of special trophies and award certificates.
- Assists in the preparation of department's annual budget.
- Administers the annual employee survey, summarizing and reporting results to the Manufacturing Manager and his staff.
- Coordinates the annual performance review process, collecting written reviews and scheduling overall reviews of each department with the Manufacturing Manager.
- Coordinates the annual salary review program for both professional and nonexempt employees, making sure reviews are completed on time and pay increase forms have been timely processed.
- Provides other administrative tasks as requested.

Katherine T. Mattings   **Page 2**

Production Scheduling Clerk   (1995 – 2000)
Reported to the Manager of Production Scheduling, providing administrative and clerical support in the production scheduling process for three manufacturing plants.

- Followed established procedures in converting monthly and quarterly sales forecasts into usable production scheduling data.
- Broke down sales forecasts by product category, volume and needed delivery times.
- Assisted Manager of Production Scheduling in the preparation of machine loan schedules and coordinated raw materials and supplies ordering from Procurement.
- Typed and emailed weekly and monthly production schedules to plant production management.
- Used production computer system to track daily production and reported schedule deviations to Manager of Production Scheduling.
- Answered phone and routed calls to members of the Department.
- Sorted and distributed Department mail.
- Performed other administrative tasks as requested by Manager of Production Scheduling.

EDUCATION

High School Diploma
Elverson High School, 1995

COMPUTER SKILLS

MS Word
Excel
PowerPoint
Access
SAS
MFG Scheduling

HAROLD B. CARTER

816 Willow Street
Philadelphia, PA 19237
Home: (602) 422-5183

Email: HarCar816@MSN.com

OBJECTIVE

Mailroom Clerk

SUMMARY

Accurate, thorough, and conscientious Mail Clerk with 5 years corporate mailroom experience in the sorting and delivery of mail in a 1,200-employee corporate office complex.

EXPERIENCE

CAMPBELL SOUP COMPANY, Camden, New Jersey   **1995 to Present**
World's leading soup manufacturer with 15 manufacturing plants and operations in over 30 countries worldwide.

Mailroom Clerk – Corporate Offices (2000 to Present)
Report to Mailroom Supervisor with responsibility for receipt, sorting, and delivery of mail in a 1,200-employee corporate office facility.

- Receives, sorts, and delivers all incoming mail, interdepartmental mail, notices, memoranda, and packages to over 35 departments and functions.
- Sorts, weighs, and affixes proper postage to all outgoing mail, delivering it to outgoing mail receptacle.
- Wraps and properly packages all outgoing boxes and packages for shipment by U.S. Mail, Federal Express, Airborne Express, and other carriers.
- Operates Pitney Bowes mailing equipment in the folding, stuffing, and mailing of bulk mail projects.
- Inventories and stocks packaging and mailing supplies including special envelopes, cartons, boxes, tape, etc.

Night Shift Janitor – Corporate Offices (1998 – 2000)
Reported to Night Shift Supervisor, with responsibility for cleaning 100,000 square foot office area.

- Collected and emptied all trash receptacles, transporting to dumpster.
- Dusted office furniture and vacuumed floors.
- Washed and waxed all office corridors.
- Washed and cleaned all restroom facilities.
- Replenished restrooms with toilet tissue, facial tissue, and towel products.

Harold B. Carter **Page 2**

- Maintained inventory of cleaning and restroom supplies.
- Assisted night shift crew in the movement and placement of office furniture.

Security Guard – Corporate Offices (1995 – 1998)
Reported to Night Shift Security Officer, with responsibility for manning the main entrance security desk during second shift operations.

- Checked all visitors for proper identification before authorizing building entry.
- Maintained visitor register, requiring sign-in by all personnel entering building.
- Used remote video surveillance equipment to monitor all building entrances and limited access areas throughout building complex.
- Rotated with other security guards in making scheduled rounds of building structure.
- Investigate and report any unusual activity suggesting security breach.

EDUCATION

High School Diploma
Camden High School, 1995

BRUCE W. WILLARD
106 North Fork Road
Landisville, NJ 19273

Phone: (609) 695-4782   Email: BruWill@AOL.com   Cell: (609) 372-1434

OBJECTIVE

Team Leader / Lead Operator / Production Supervisor

SUMMARY

Well-trained, skilled and spirited team leader / production supervisor with demonstrated skill in energizing and motivating workers to meet and/or exceed productivity goals and set production records. Solid communications, interpersonal, and leadership skills. Enjoy the challenge of building and leading in a team-based environment.

EXPERIENCE

JOHNSON & JOHNSON, Landisville, NJ Plant   **1996 to Present**
A world-leading manufacturer of over-the-counter and proprietary drug products.

Production Team Leader (2000 to Present)
Report to Shift Operations Manager with responsibility for maintaining and improving high-speed packaging line performance in order to meet and exceed budgeted production and reliability goals.

- Organize daily operations for work team and ensure work area cleanliness.
- Communicate daily with production planners, product compounding, and analytical lab to meet reliability goals.
- Train in team-based work systems and coach new workers throughout learning process.
- Conduct behavior-based interviews in selection of workers compatible with team-based work culture.
- Organize training schedules to cross train workers in multiple skill positions.
- Ensure maximum utilization of assigned personnel, equipment, and materials to meet scheduled production rates.
- Motivate and encourage employees to participate in self-initiated continuous improvement initiates designed to improve production line efficiency and reduce operating expense.
- Maintain espirit de corps and high employee morale through personal encouragement and recognition for achievement.
- Monitor employee skill levels and encourage employees to undertake appropriate training to reach full potential and prepare for career progression and advancement.
- Set example through good work habits and contribute to team spirit and high morale.

Line Operator & Material Handler (1996 – 2000)
Reported to Packaging Team Leader with responsibility for efficiently operating high-speed packaging equipment and achieving both production and quality goals.

- Managed packaging technical methods and operated packaging equipment.
- Supplied production line with raw materials (bottles, cartons, and containers).

Bruce W. Willard   **Page 2**

- Managed inventory systems.
- Followed safe practices to ensure that GMP and federal standards were met.

EDUCATION

High School Diploma
North Penn High School, 1996

COMPANY TRAINING

Leadership Training
Total Quality
Confrontation Skills
Good Manufacturing Practices
HPI Computer System
Mechanical Skills
Basic Hand Tools

WANDA B. JOHNSON
700 East 7th Street
Lansdale, PA 19346
Phone: (610) 775-0984
Email: WanJo7 @AOL.com

OBJECTIVE

Machine Operator / Lead Operator / Production Worker

SUMMARY

Efficient, hard-working lead machine operator / production worker with 19 years of production experience in a food manufacturing and processing plant. Demonstrated leadership and machine operating skills in a team-based production environment. Strong mechanical troubleshooting competencies combined with excellent communications and interpersonal skills.

EXPERIENCE

CLARKSON MANUFACTURING, INC., Willow Grove, PA Plant   **1986 to Present**
A 500-employee manufacturing facility engaged in the production and processing of consumer food products including cake mixes, packaged soups, salad dressing, coffee, and miscellaneous condiments.

Lead Operator – Salad Dressing (1998 to Present)
Report to Operations Shift Supervisor with responsibility for functioning as the Lead Operator of a salad dressing production line including formulation, mixing, filling, and packing operations.

- Train and oversee the daily production of 8 to 10 production line workers.
- Ensure achievement of production goals and maintenance of quality standards.
- Coach and train new employees on filler, cartoner, and HPI computer operation as well as safe operating procedures and quality standards.
- Provide basic troubleshooting ensuring rapid repair and minimum line downtime.
- Operate equipment as needed to replace employees on break or absent due to illness.
- Analyze downtime tracking to eliminate causes and improve line productivity.
- Maintain and submit required production records and reports.
- Attend shift change meetings to ensure smooth transition to oncoming shift personnel.
- File safety and accident reports.
- Participate as member of Plant Safety Committee.

Production Worker – Salad Dressing (1986 – 1998)
Reported to Lead Operator with responsibility for efficiently running a high-speed salad dressing filling and cartoning operation.

- Operated packaging machinery (fillers and cartoner), following required safety procedures, and ensuring that production goals and company quality standards were achieved.

- Utilized histograms to monitor fill levels and off torques, and performed quality checks throughout shift to meet GMP standards.
- Entered data into computer system to record material movement, inventory tracking, finished product forecasting, and individual productivity.
- Received "Top Gun Award" for achieving over 85% process reliability for 3 consecutive months.
- Achieved plant record for "rapid changeover" (15 minutes versus 30 minute plant average).

EDUCATION

High School Diploma
North Penn High School, 1986

COMPANY TRAINING

Good Manufacturing Practices
Total Quality
Forklift Truck Operation
Basic Hand Tools
Job Safety
Computer Basics

LINDA A. BAXTER
222 Greenfield Circle
Little Rock, AK 23130
Phone: (714) 552-9751
Email: LinBax22 @AOL.com

OBJECTIVE

Production Worker

SUMMARY

Dedicated, conscientious production worker who takes pride in the quality of her work. Over six years experience working in a variety of positions in a chemical process environment. Enjoy working as a team member in a participative environment where employees are charged with the responsibility for improving the effectiveness and efficiency of operations.

EXPERIENCE

THE RAYBURN CORPORATION, Fort Smith, AK   **1998 to Present**
A 575-employee chemical manufacturing facility, providing chemical intermediates to the pharmaceutical and food industries.

Lead Operator (2003 to Present)
Report to Operations Shift Manager with responsibility for providing leadership to a crew of 8 employees engaged in the weighing, batching, and mixing of specialty chemicals in accordance with prescribed batch recipes and required operating procedures.

- Provide daily guidance and leadership to a team of 8 production workers to ensure production goals and schedules are met.
- Monitor quality and safety standards, taking corrective action as needed.
- Train new crewmembers in basic job skills and proper use of materials and equipment.
- Conduct shift-change meetings to ensure continuity of operations.
- Troubleshoot causes of out-of-specification product, taking required remedial action.
- Developed team training program for making and weighing operations to improve operator skills.
- Implemented security location system to ensure proper storage, improve ease of access, and reduce weighing times in chemical make-up area.
- Developed critical path to improve overall efficiency of batch-making process.
- Led redesign and modification of wastewater sanitizing system, reducing waste water processing costs by $ 25,000 monthly.

Batch Maker (2001 – 2003)
Reported to Lead Operator with responsibility for chemical batch make-up in accordance with prescribed recipe and formulation instructions.

- Weighed and blended chemical compounds in proper ratios in preparation for mixing operations.
- Maintained accuracy and timeliness of all batch production records.
- Cleaned and sanitized all production equipment to ensure integrity of product.
- Adhered to all GMP, safety, and standard operating procedure guidelines.

Warehouse Worker (1998 – 2001)
Reported to Warehouse Shift Leader with responsibility for performing a variety of warehouse duties in connection with receipt, storage, and delivery of raw materials and vital supplies to production operations.

- Operated forklift trucks and palletizing equipment.
- Removed material from trailers and stored in warehouse locations.
- Ordered supplies from warehouse using computerized pick list.
- Performed weekly maintenance of warehouse equipment.

EDUCATION

High School Diploma
Souder's Creek High School, 1988

COMPANY TRAINING

Forklift Truck Operation
Compounding
Inventory Control
Basic Leadership
G.M.P.
S.O.P.

DONALD R. FREEMAN

605 North Ridge Road
Appleton, WI 13486
Phone: (402) 663-0978
Email: DRFree@MSN.com

OBJECTIVE

Machine Tender – Paper Machine

SUMMARY

Skilled Machine Tender with seventeen years experience in the operation of 3,000 feet-per-minute, high-speed tissue paper machine (80 tons per day). Background includes paper machine start-up and training of new crews including Back Tenders, Third Hand, and First Hand. Experienced in use of computer process control systems including Honeywell TDC 3000 and related instrumentation. Solid leadership, interpersonal, and communications skills.

EXPERIENCE

FOSTER PAPER COMPANY, INC., Marinette, WI   **1984 to Present**
The Marinette paper plant employs 1,015 employees and manufactures, converts and finishes consumer tissue and towel products including facial tissue, toilet tissue, and paper hand towels.

Machine Tender – # 8 Paper Machine (2000 to Present)
Report to Paper Mill Shift Supervisor. Oversee 4-person papermaking team in the operation of a 3,000 feet-per-minute, 80 ton-per-day tissue paper machine.

- Leads 4-person paper machine crew in the production of jumbo parent rolls used in the manufacture, converting, and finishing of consumer toilet tissue products.
- Exercises complete machine operating responsibility for this 100-yard long machine, from head box through reel.
- Trains support crew (Back Hand, Third Hand, & First Hand) in proper operating procedures in operation of their respective machine sections.
- Uses machine control panel to continuously monitor and control all machine sections for variances in speed, temperature, pressure, and flow, overriding automated controls and making manual adjustments as required.
- Maintains paper machine within established control parameters to ensure efficient operation and consistent quality of finished product.
- Ensures machine crew is thoroughly trained in safe operating procedures and strictly adheres to safety rules and regulations at all times.
- Served as lead operator during the highly successful rebuild and start-up of the # 8 paper machine, beating productivity goals by 20% in first year of operation.
- Awarded the Paper Mill Superintendent's "Top Gun Award" in 2000, 2002, 2003, and 2004, as the top producing paper machine in the mill.

Back Hand – # 8 Paper Machine (1989 – 2000)
Reported to Machine Tender - # 8 Paper Machine with responsibility for operation of the machine's calendar stack and reel sections.

- Operated overhead lift in removing finished parent rolls from the reel section for delivery to paper converting and finishing operations.

Donald R. Freeman   Page 2

- Ensured smooth transfer of paper to new cores, following removal of finished parent roll, avoiding costly paper breaks and mountains of paper broke.
- Oversaw First Hand in the threading of machine following paper breaks and machine start-ups.
- Trained First Hand in calendar stack and reel operation as relief person during Back Tender absences and in preparation for move-up.

First Hand - # 8 Paper Machine (1986 – 1989)
Reported to Machine Tender - # 8 Paper Machine, providing operating support and performing miscellaneous duties as directed.

- Threaded paper machine following paper breaks and during machine start-ups.
- Fed broke into machine broke chest following machine paper breaks.
- Assisted Back Tender in removal of completed parent rolls from back-stand and transported them to converting operations.
- Provided miscellaneous duties as directed by Machine Tender and Back Hand.

Materials Handler – Towel Finishing (1984 – 1986)
Reported to Shift Supervisor with responsibility for supplying towel converting and finishing operations with raw materials and vital supplies.

- Operated forklift truck in the delivery of paper stock parent rolls to towel converting operations.
- Used electric hand truck to deliver packaging materials and vital supplies from warehouse to finishing unit.
- Assisted re-winder operator in loading parent roll stock on to re-winder back-stand.
- Delivered and stacked corrugated knockdowns for use in case packer.

EDUCATION

High School Diploma
Appleton High School, 1984

COMPANY TRAINING

Paper Machine Operation
Machine Controls – Honeywell TDC 3000
Total Quality Control
Safe Manufacturing Practices
Forklift Truck Operation
Electric Hand Truck Operation
Good Manufacturing Practices

JOHN P. BRANSON
25 Woodlawn Circle
Huron, OH 18347
Home: (205) 663-9574

Email: JoBran25@AOL.com

OBJECTIVE

Machine Operator / Production Worker - Manufacturing

SUMMARY

Industrious, efficient, and dedicated Machine Operator / Production Worker with over 10 years experience working in a high performance, team-oriented manufacturing environment. Excellent training in modern production methods and practices, including lean manufacturing, total quality, statistical process control, and mechanical troubleshooting.

EXPERIENCE

SCOTT PAPER COMPANY, INC., Sandusky, OH Plant   **1991 to Present**
A $5.2 billion, leading manufacturer of consumer paper products including facial tissue, toilet tissue, napkins, and towels.

Team Leader – Shop Towels (2002 to Present)
Report to Shift Manufacturing Manger with responsibility for leading a 3-person team in the manufacture of new state-of-the-art, disposable shop towel.

- Oversees daily shift operation of finishing line including air lay process, web formation, winder, re-winder, and Lennox sheeter operation.
- Provides daily direction and guidance to 3-person crew in meeting daily production and quality goals.
- Coordinates with Vital Supplies to ensure the delivery of sufficient raw material fiber, adhesive, sleeves, and cartons to support continuous shift operations and avoid unscheduled downtime.
- Provides routine troubleshooting and repair of equipment to maintain production goals and schedules.
- Coordinates with Quality Lab to track down and troubleshoot quality problems, initiating rapid corrective action to minimize product waste.
- Provides daily inspection and audit of equipment and operations for preventive maintenance purposes.
- Ensures maintenance schedules are met, and line is kept in peak operating condition.
- Trains new operators in proper manufacturing and safe operating methods and procedures.
- Exceeded shift productivity goals by 15% over a 6-month period.
- Set plant production record, winning inter-shift competition and "Top Gun Award" in 2004.

John P. Branson   **Page 2**

Production Associate – Shop Towels (2000 to 2002)
Reported to Team Leader as part of a 3-person, high performance team responsible for the start-up and operation of company's Shop Towel manufacturing line.

- Operated Lennox sheeter in the slitting, sheeting, and finishing of Shop Towel product.
- Provided mechanical troubleshooting and repair to sheeter and entire production line.
- Served as key member of start-up team that successfully started up first-ever Shop Towel production line.
- Shattered start-up production goals, reaching first year's volume goal in only 6 months.
- Won inter-shift competition 5 out of 6 months, turning in highest production volume and setting plant all-time record.
- Trained as part of company's first high performance manufacturing work team.
- Crossed trained in Rando webber, Rando feeder, and oven operation.
- Rotated through all line jobs on a monthly basis

Bag Machine Leader – Cutrite Wax Paper   (1995 – 2000)
Bag Machine Operator – Cutrite Wax Paper   (1992 – 1995)
Roll Transporter – Waxer Operations   (1991 – 1992)

EDUCATION

High School Diploma
Sandusky High School, 1991

COMPANY TRAINING

High Performance Work Teams
Total Quality
Statistical Process Control
Lean Manufacturing
Basic Hand Tools
Mechanical Troubleshooting
Safe Manufacturing Practices

CORA B. WILSON
235 Windsor Road
Winslow, ME 12385
Phone: (321) 775-0928
Email: CorWil@AOL.com

OBJECTIVE

Mechanical Adjuster

SUMMARY

Skilled Mechanical Adjuster, able to make rapid mechanical adjustments "on the run", keeping production lines operating efficiently with little or no unscheduled downtime. Talented troubleshooter with solid mechanical skills and the ability to isolate and identify machine failures quickly and initiate immediate corrective action. Also trained in basic electrical troubleshooting and repair.

EXPERIENCE

WHEATLY PAPER COMPANY, INC., Winslow, ME   **1994 to Present**
The Winslow paper plant employs 820 employees and manufactures, converts and finishes consumer grades of tissue and towel products. Products include toiler tissue, facial tissue, napkins, and roll towels.

Mechanical Adjuster – Towel Finishing (2003 to Present)
Report to Towel Department Shift Supervisor with accountability for providing production line mechanical troubleshooting and repair in support of towel converting and finishing operations. Support 4 lines of high-speed, electro-mechanical equipment including re-winders, slitters, poly-wrappers, unitizers, case-packers/sealers, and barcode printers.

- Provides quick diagnosis and rapid mechanical repair to high-speed, integrated paper converting, finishing, and packaging lines, minimizing production downtime and product waste.
- Maintains complete and accurate records of all repairs as the basis for predictive and preventive maintenance program development.
- Fine-tunes sensitive electro-mechanical adjustments involving split-second timing and close tolerance settings.
- Performs daily shift audits and inspections of all equipment to spot and anticipate mechanical failures before they occur.
- Carries out scheduled maintenance in accordance with preventive maintenance program schedule.
- Ensures that Stores maintains proper inventory levels of critical machine parts to avoid delays and minimize unscheduled downtime.
- Provides basic electrical troubleshooting and repair, as needed.
- Ensures the proper installation and immediate repair of all machine guards and related safety equipment to protect employees and prevent injury.

Re-winder Operator – Towel Finishing (1998 – 2003)
Reported to Shift Supervisor with responsibility for operation of a re-winder in the manufacture of consumer roll towels.

- Responsible for the safe and efficient operation of a high-speed paper towel re-winder / slitter in meeting production and quality goals.
- Ensured adequate supply of base stock parent rolls to support shift production requirements.

- Closely observed tail-gluing operation to ensure proper glue consistency and application, avoiding product rejection and waste.
- Continuously checked for quality issues such as poor perforations and printing off-registration, taking remedial action as appropriate.
- Performed minor machine troubleshooting and repair as needed.
- Followed safe operating practices.
- Relieved case-sealer operator during re-winder cross-training.

Materials Handler – Towel Finishing (1994 – 1998)
Reported to Shift Supervisor with responsibility for supplying towel converting and finishing operations with raw materials and vital supplies.

- Operated forklift truck in the delivery of paper stock parent rolls to towel converting operations.
- Used electric hand truck to deliver packaging materials and vital supplies from warehouse to finishing unit.
- Assisted re-winder operator in loading parent roll stock on to re-winder back-stand.
- Delivered and stacked corrugated knockdowns for use in case packer.

EDUCATION

High School Diploma
Winslow High School, 1994

COMPANY TRAINING

Forklift Truck Operation
Electric Hand Truck Operation
Inventory Control Procedures
Good Manufacturing Practices
Re-Winder Operator Training
Safe Manufacturing Practices

WILLIAM R. KLEIN
1514 Brainerd Street
Cincinnati, OH 13286
Phone: (712) 345-5514

OBJECTIVE

Painter / Drywall Installer

SUMMARY

Skilled Sheet Metal Fabricator / Metal Worker with experience in the fabrication of heating and air conditioning systems. Hard-working, conscientious employee who takes pride in his work and is committed to quality craftsmanship.

EXPERIENCE

MORTON HVAC SYSTEMS, INC., Cincinnati, OH   **2001 to Present**
Manufacturer and fabricator of heating and air conditioning systems for residential and commercial applications.

Sheet Metal Fabricator
Reports to Fabrication Supervisor with responsibility for the sheet metal fabrication of the ductwork and metal housing of residential and commercial heating and air conditioning systems.

- Develops layout and plans sequence of operations for the cutting, fabrication, and assembly of sheet metal ductwork for heating and air conditioning assemblies.
- Uses mathematical skills and knowledge of metal to plan work layout.
- Locates and marks bending and cutting lines onto work piece.
- Allows for stock thickness and machine and welding shrinkage.
- Sets up and operates fabricating equipment including breaks, rolls, shears, drill presses.
- Positions, aligns, fits, and welds parts together using jigs, welding torch, and hand tools.

EDUCATION

Certificate – Metal Working
Webster Trade School, 2001

High School Diploma
Cincinnati High School, 2000

SKILLS & ABILITIES

Metal Working / Metal Fabrication
Operation of Breaks, Rolls, Shears, and Drill Presses
Use of Jigs, Welding Torch, and Hand Tools
Basic Math

CAROLYN A. CRISWELL

407 East 7th Street
Lansdale, PA 19228
Phone: (610) 495-0244
Email: CarCris40@AOL.com

OBJECTIVE

Production Worker

SUMMARY

Hardworking, conscientious production worker experienced in pharmaceutical manufacturing in a team-based, high-performance work system environment. Skills include bulk product formulation, line maintenance, warehousing operations, line troubleshooting, and forklift truck operations.

EXPERIENCE

BRIGHTON PHARMACEUTICALS, INC., Lansdale, PA   **1998 to Present**
The Lansdale plant operates as a team-based, high-performance work system operation, manufacturing over-the-counter pharmaceutical and consumer personal products (i.e., hand lotions, shampoos, hair care products, toothpaste, and denture cream).

Compounder – Pharmaceutical Products (2002 to Present)
Report to Operations Shift Manager with responsibility for compounding products in accordance with prescribed formulation and approved operating procedures.

- Precisely weigh raw materials for batch preparation to ensure consistency and high-quality production.
- Retrieve chemicals through computerized HPI system to determine availability, approval, and location.
- Adhere to strict compliance with GMP regulations for chemical lot control and to ensure timely product supply.
- Clean and sanitize production equipment to prevent contamination and guarantee product integrity.

Production Worker (1998 – 2002)
Reported to Shift Supervisor with responsibility, as a team member, for operation of a high-speed pharmaceutical packaging production line.

- Responsible for operation of a high-speed packaging line in a team-based, high-performance work system environment.
- Job duties include equipment operation, equipment adjustment for product changeovers, quality assurance, label review, and data input into production computer system.
- Train new team members in effective equipment operation and standard operating procedures.
- Ensure production line has required inventory when needed, including picking and delivering needed items from warehouse.
- Responsible for meeting quality control standards and production schedules.
- Inspect and sample raw material and packaging supplies to ensure conformance to government standards.
- Operate various materials handling equipment including forklift trucks, electric hand trucks, and jacks during material transport to production areas.

- Operate computerized swing-reach equipment to retrieve stored materials from automated warehouse operation.
- Ensure production line is stocked with adequate supplies of caps, bottles, tubes, and containers to prevent production delays and avoid line downtime.
- Ensure FDA compliance in warehouse operations through accurate identification of raw materials and packaging materials prior to entry into production line inventory.
- Load and unload trailers, moving tote trucks and trash bins.

EDUCATION

High School Diploma
North Penn High School, 1998

COMPANY TRAINING

Forklift Truck Operation
Total Quality Control
Inventory Control
Good Manufacturing Practices
Working Safely
Basic Hand Tools
Basic Mechanical Troubleshooting

WILLIAM H. HARBSTER
123 Puritan Way
Wilbraham, MA 13824
Phone: (607) 277-5431
Email: WilHarb@AOL.com

OBJECTIVE

Electrical and Instrument Technician

SUMMARY

Highly motivated, team-oriented Electrical and Instrument Technician with extensive experience in high-speed, automated packaging lines and general utilities equipped with PLC's. Self-starter who learns quickly and performs well both independently and in a team environment.

EXPERIENCE

TAYLOR PACKAGING, INC., Springfield, MA   **1996 to Present**
This packaging plant employs 175 employees and provides contract-packaging services to a number of leading consumer and commercial product manufacturing companies.

Electrical & Instrumentation Technician (2004 - Present)
Report to Electrical Maintenance Supervisor with responsibility for providing installation, maintenance, troubleshooting, and repair of instrumentation and control systems on high-speed packaging lines.

- Perform troubleshooting, preventive maintenance, and project installation work in the application of instrumentation and controls to high-speed mechanical equipment.
- Assist line operators and engineers in center-lining production equipment through the installation of automatic timers and counters to accurately monitor production efficiencies and reduce downtime.
- Assist production engineers in the design and start-up of new packaging lines in accordance with company design standards for instrumentation and controls.
- Apply comprehensive knowledge of PLC/line interface to troubleshoot electrical line controls including Vision Systems.
- Participate with engineers and project managers during project update meetings with engineering management and plant staff.

Packaging Line Operator (1996 – 2004)
Reported to Packing Line Leader with responsibility for operating packaging equipment to achieve department production and reliability goals.

- Rotated through various packaging line positions to gain first-hand knowledge of equipment and its operation.
- Performed all line duties and quickly learned use of changeover area equipment to reduce downtime.
- Learned to use histograms to monitor fill levels and off torques.
- Performed quality checks throughout shift.

EDUCATION

High School Diploma
Springfield High School, 1996

Springfield Vo-Tech School
Courses in Basic Electrical Troubleshooting & Repair

COMPANY TRAINING

PLC-5 Programming & Troubleshooting
Electronics and Computer Programming
Allen Bradley Co. – PLC Training
Rumsey Electric Co. – PLC Training and Hardwire
Statistical Process Control
Safe Practices Seminar

DAVID P. BIREN
625 Forrester Lane
Dayton, OH 19736

Home: (206) 773-9992   Email: DaBir625@MSN.com   Cell: (206) 752-1238

OBJECTIVE

Mechanic – Manufacturing Company

SUMMARY

Efficient, motivated production line mechanic with extensive experience in the installation and start-up of new packaging line equipment, including operator training, safety, reliability and ergonomics. Known as a self-starter who learns quickly and functions effectively in a team environment. Strong technical, communications, and interpersonal skills.

EXPERIENCE

WILSON MANUFACTURING, INC., Dayton, OH   **2000 to Present**
This 375-employee plant manufactures a wide range of household cleaning products including detergents, bleaches, window cleaners, polishes, and cleansing agents.

Packaging Line Mechanic
Report to Packaging Line Supervisor with responsibility for providing mechanical maintenance, troubleshooting, and repair to support the efficient, continuous running of packaging equipment and minimize line downtime.

- Functioned as lead mechanic in the successful installation and start-up of new bottling and tube filling lines.
- Responsible for all mechanical aspects of new $2 MM production line to include machinery specification, installation, start-up, and subsequent maintenance and troubleshooting of same.
- Implemented and maintained machine centerline used to achieve quick product changeovers and reduce need for fine-tuning.
- Improved functioning of line equipment to meet rapid changeover demands.
- Reduced unscheduled downtime from 2 hours to 20 minutes per shift through use of downtime tracking system, equipment modification, and creative teaming with equipment vendor.
- Used troubleshooting skills and creative resources to increase process reliability from 80% to 90% in four-month period.
- Designed and implemented area maintenance systems that were subsequently adopted as the model for all lines in plant.
- Assisted in the design, construction, and start-up of new packaging line, including Commission Qualification Verification acceptance criteria for new equipment.
- Consistently met and exceeded line process and efficiency goals through implementation of Single Minute Exchange of Dies techniques, and training of line operators in basic maintenance and troubleshooting.
- Frequently participate in meetings with plant management to review and update progress of project work, line reliability, etc.

David P. Biren **Page 2**

TEMPCO EQUIPMENT COMPANY, Dayton, OH **1996 - 2000**
Manufacturer of custom packaging equipment for use in the packaging of a wide range of consumer and commercial products.

Packaging Mechanic
Reported to Project Engineer with responsibility for installation, start-up, debugging, and fine-tuning of new packaging line installations at customer manufacturing facilities.

- Set-up and debugged packaging equipment installations.
- Trained customer employees in equipment operation and maintenance.
- Provided emergency troubleshooting and repair services to customers as needed.

EDUCATION

High School Diploma
Dayton High School, 1996

Dayton Technical Institute
Coursework in machine design, mechanical drafting,
basic mechanics, and mechanical troubleshooting & repair.

COMPANY TRAINING

Centerline Quick Changeover
Vendor Machine Training
Video Jet Coders
SMED
Preventive Maintenance
OSHA Compliance

PETER M. BRISTOL

116 Green Ridge Road
Muskegon, MI 23440

Home: (217) 874-2237   Email: PeBri116@AOL.com   Cell: (217) 872-5514

OBJECTIVE

Operating Engineer – Plant Utilities

SUMMARY

Knowledgeable, skilled Utilities Engineer with more than five years experience in the installation, operation, repair, and troubleshooting of plant utility systems (i.e., boilers, steam, heat, water, and air supplies) in support of plant operations. Dedicated, efficient and productive worker noted for being responsive and decisive during utility emergencies. Conscientious, reliable, and solid team player.

EXPERIENCE

PAPER CONVERTING, INC., Muskegon, MI   **1999 to Present**
This 175 worker plant converts paper parent roll stock into consumer tissue products including facial tissue, toilet tissue, and napkins for private label distributors.

Operating Engineer - Utilities (2000 to Present)
Report to Plant Maintenance Supervisor with responsibility for providing plant operations with all process utilities including heat, steam, water, and air supplies.

- Responsible for operation and maintenance of plant steam, compressed air, USP purified water, HVAC, fire protection, water treatment, energy management, and chilled water systems.
- Maintains, troubleshoots, and repairs utility systems to meet all plant operation needs and avoid unnecessary line shutdowns.
- Operates and maintains boilers in a manner that ensures the safety and well-being of employees and safeguards plant assets.
- Led project to replace plant air compressors and upgrade compressed air system resulting in $30,000 annual cost savings.
- Developed skills in project management, plumbing, pipefitting, and electrical troubleshooting.
- Lead member of 3-person energy project team that upgraded HVAC system resulting in energy savings of $40,000 annually.
- Teamed with Wisconsin Electric Company to redesign chilled water system, reducing energy costs by $ 25,000 per year.

Production Worker/Machine Operator (1999 – 2000)
Worked in various plant operating assignments including the finishing & converting, shipping and receiving departments.

- Ran Lennox sheeter/slitter in the manufacture of disposable shop towels.
- Machine operator of intermittent winder in the production of toilet tissue.
- Operated facial tissue finishing and packaging line, including poly-wrap, carton machine, and case sealing operations.

- Functioned as Adjuster (shift mechanic) on second shift of tissue finishing operation.
- Worked as Forklift Operator in the Distribution Center.
- Loaded tractor-trailers and boxcars in Shipping Department.

EDUCATION

High School Diploma
Muskegon High School, 1996

TRAINING & CERTIFICATIONS

State of Wisconsin	-	Class A Engineer License
Muskegon Technical Institute	-	Industrial Motors & Controls
		Boiler Operations & Controls
		Refrigeration & Air Conditioning (1, 2, & 3)
		Industrial Electricity (1&2)
Fireman's Mutual Insurance	-	Fire Production
Company Seminars	-	OSHA Compliance
		Total Quality
		Safe Operating Practices

GREGORY W. DODD
426 Piney Brooke Road
Green Bay, WI 23960

Home: (616) 335-0047   Email: GreDo@AOL.com   Cell: (206) 752-1238

OBJECTIVE

Electrician – Manufacturing Company

SUMMARY

Skilled electrician with over 15 years experience in the installation, start-up, troubleshooting, repair, and maintenance of electric power and power distribution systems in a manufacturing environment. Efficient, hardworking, dedicated worker with excellent interpersonal and communications skills. Solid team player who can also work independently with little or no supervision.

EXPERIENCE

WISCONSIN FOODS, INC., Appleton, WI   **2000 to Present**
This 600-employee food manufacturing and processing facility produces cereals, crackers, cookies, cheeses, and other dairy-related food products.

Electrician
Report to Electrical Maintenance Leader with responsibility for providing electrical installation, maintenance, troubleshooting, and repair in support of manufacturing and utility operations.

- Provide electrical maintenance, installation, and troubleshooting for all plant utility and general building areas, including fire system pump houses.
- Provide electrical maintenance and troubleshooting support to all production and packaging operations.
- Repair and maintain electric motors and gearboxes, including bearing replacement, shaft replacement, and winding repair.
- Maintain and troubleshoot electrical supply for all plant HVAC, boiler, and utility operations.
- Provide electrical maintenance support to engineering project teams in the installation and/or rebuild of production lines.
- Oversee work of electrical contractors during major rebuilds and installations.

TRI-STATE EQUIPMENT COMPANY, Green Bay, WI   **1988 - 2000**
Electrical contract firm providing installation, troubleshooting, and repair support to utility companies in the tri-state area.

Electrician

- Installed, maintained, and performed electrical troubleshooting for oil and gas companies.
- Extensive experience running conduit and wiring in explosion-proof areas.

EDUCATION

High School Diploma
Marinette High School, 1986

Green Bay Technical Institute, Industrial Electricity, 1987 - 1988
National Electrical Code and N.F.P.A., Training Seminar, 1988

MATTHEW R. FOX

206 Devon Terrace
Douglassville, PA 19238

Home: (610) 877-5324   Email: RedFox20@MSN.com   Cell: (610) 877-5948

OBJECTIVE

Maintenance Leader / Lead Mechanic

SUMMARY

Multi-skilled Maintenance Leader / Lead Mechanic with 15+ years hands-on and leadership experience in the maintenance of a wide range of production lines, equipment, and buildings. Played key role in a number of line rebuilds, installations, and capital improvement projects. Noted for creative solutions to challenging mechanical problems. Solid leadership, interpersonal, and communication skills.

EXPERIENCE

DARLENE COSMETICS, INC., Reading, PA   **1980 to Present**
A leading manufacturer of women's cosmetics and men's toiletry products, this 800-employee plant facility operates as a "high-performance work system" operation. It is a team-based environment with focus on individual development and the full utilization of the skills and abilities of its workforce.

Plant Maintenance Leader (2000 to Present)
Report to Operations Manager and charged with the responsibility to improve overall maintenance efficiency while simultaneously enhancing Operation's ability to meet and/or exceed production goals.

- Manage, maintain, and update plant's computerized Preventive Maintenance Program.
- Key contributor to the successful design and start-up of a $3 million production line and related packaging operation, including development and implementation of standards and procedures for equipment acceptance (e.g., PSI, CQV, Project Management).
- Used data from downtime tracking system to eliminate key causes of unscheduled downtime, reducing line downtime from 2 hours to 20 minutes per shift (avoiding $200,000 rebuild).
- Provided training, timelines, models, and goals for new maintenance programs to be used in packaging and process areas of the plant (e.g., T.P.M., oil analysis, thermal, ultrasonic, etc.).
- Participate in meetings and presentations to review and update project status at the team, plant, and corporate levels.

Packaging Line Mechanic (1994 – 2000)
Reported to Packaging Operations Manager, serving as chief shift mechanic in the maintenance, troubleshooting, and repair of 5 packaging lines.

- Performed troubleshooting, changeovers, equipment rebuilds, preventive & predictive maintenance, and operating improvement project work.
- Provided effective electrical troubleshooting support to line operations through solid understanding of PLC interface with line equipment and electrical controls.
- Increased process reliability from 70% to 80% in three months, while simultaneously meeting or exceeding safety goals.

- Worked closely with packaging material vendors to resolve problems and recommend improvements.

Building Maintenance Mechanic (1989 – 1994)
Reported to Maintenance Manager with responsibility for maintaining building appearance and function. Performed carpentry, masonry, tile installation, and other miscellaneous work related to building upkeep.

Production Worker – Q.C. Inspector, Machine Operator, Material Handler (1980 – 1989)
Worked in a variety of plant jobs prior to pursuing Maintenance career.

EDUCATION

Reading Technological Institute
Packaging & Converting Machine Mechanic, 1990

High School Diploma
Douglasville High School, 1980

COMPANY TRAINING

Allen Bradley PLC Basic
PLC Maintenance & Troubleshooting
Total Quality Management
Project Management & Leadership
OSHA Compliance
Quality Windows
Microsoft Office – Word, Excel, PowerPoint

ROBERT J. LLOYD
526 North 5th Street
Jacksonville, FL 12837
Phone: (326) 422-7596
Email: RoLloy@AOL.com

OBJECTIVE

Storeroom Clerk

SUMMARY

Knowledgeable, conscientious Storeroom Clerk with extensive experience in the stocking, supply and efficient management of storeroom operations. Familiar with preventive and predictive maintenance concepts, and skilled at establishing parts stocking strategies designed to minimize inventory investment while simultaneously preventing out-of-stock emergencies and machine downtime.

EXPERIENCE

STARBRITE MANUFACTURING COMPANY, INC., Jacksonville, FL Plant   **1997 to Present**
A 900-employee manufacturing plant producing aftermarket automotive parts sold through a nationwide network of private label parts distributors, major auto repair shops and car dealerships.

Storeroom Clerk (2001 – Present)
Report to Plant Maintenance Manager with responsibility for overseeing the stocking and daily operation of an 8,000 item plant storeroom facility.

- Reorganized storeroom layout by production department, facilitating ease of replacement part stocking and facilitating parts location during second and third shift operations.
- Carefully tracked parts usage over 5-year period, adjusting parts stocking levels and reducing inventory investment by $ 45,000 annually.
- Assisted in the installation and set-up of computerized stores inventory tacking and re-order entry system, designed to automatically order standard parts when parts inventory levels drop to established reorder points.
- Trained Maintenance personnel and Manufacturing Shift Supervisors in use of computerized inventory tracking system to track parts withdrawal using barcode scanning technology.
- Initiated use of electronically coded identification cards restricting access and tracking of all personnel entering storeroom facility.
- Implemented a parts checkout process, using a combination of identification card scanning combined with parts bar code scanning, and resulting in a 50% reduction in parts "shrinkage" saving $20,000 annually.
- Catalogues, barcodes, and enters new parts into storeroom inventory.
- Reconciles parts purchase orders with deliveries, and authorizes vendor invoice payment.
- Works with Procurement to identify vendors offering improved pricing and delivery service.
- Serves as a member of the Plant Operations Effectiveness Committee.
- Serves as Chairperson of the Plant Safety Committee.

Case Packer Operator (1997 – 2001)
Reported to Manufacturing Shift Supervisor with responsibility for running a case packer in the automatic unitizing and packing of finished product into corrugated shipping cases.

- Served as Second Shift Case Packer Operator in the automatic packing of aftermarket automotive parts.
- Operated product unitizer and automatic case packer equipment, ensuring the proper packing, sealing and coding of corrugated shipping cases with finished product.
- Ensured proper operation of equipment, making online adjustments and minor repairs as needed.
- Provided routine maintenance on equipment during line shutdowns and product changeovers.
- Worked with Shift Mechanic to fine-tune machine centerline settings to improve equipment operating efficiency, enhance quality and reduce scrap.

EDUCATION

High School Diploma
Jacksonville High School, 1997

COMPANY TRAINING

Automated Inventory Control
Basic Preventive Maintenance
Basic Predictive Maintenance
Total Quality
Statistical Process Control

JAMES C. BACON
122 Green Meadow Lane
Nashville, TN 12385

Home: (512) 355-3926   Email: JaBac122@AOL.com   Cell: (512) 355-3295

OBJECTIVE

Electrical / Electronics Systems Maintenance

SUMMARY

Skilled Electrician / Electronic Systems Technician with 8+ years manufacturing maintenance experience in electrical systems. Strong background in power distribution, DC drives, variable frequency AC drives, and PLC programming. Skilled in the repair and maintenance of electronic / pneumatic controls and distributive control systems. Solid interpersonal and communication skills.

EXPERIENCE

HOBART MANUFACTURING, INC., Nashville, TN Plant   **2000 to Present**
The Nashville plant is a 600-employee, team-based manufacturing plant that produces automotive parts including gears, brakes, alternators, and generators.

Maintenance Electrician
Report to Electrical Maintenance Supervisor with responsibility for providing electrical installation, maintenance, and troubleshooting support to manufacturing operations.

- Rebuild and install industrial motors and motor controls.
- Install electronic and pneumatic control panels and control systems.
- Maintain, install, and troubleshoot hydraulic systems, compressors, conveyors, and pumps.
- Install wiring for multi-voltage motors.
- Install, troubleshoot, and repair air conditioning, alarm, and intercom systems.

WILSTON MACHINERY COMPANY, INC., Nashville, TN   **1997 to 2000**
Leading manufacturer of specialty fasteners supplied to the aircraft and aerospace industries.

Maintenance Electrician
Reported to Maintenance Superintendent with responsibility for the installation, maintenance, troubleshooting, and rebuild of presses and related equipment.

- Redesigned and rebuilt Ransom P2 presses, including computerization of controls.
- Replaced manual controls with solid-state computer controls, coupled with inductive proximity and fiber optic systems.
- Outfitted uncoilers with solid-state programmable variable drive controls, and box conveyors with GE Junior 1 computer systems, both interfacing with main press computer.
- Built electronic controllers for automatic timed compound extruders, using 555 solid-state timer chips and multi-speed vibrator controls, built on edge cards for easy replacement.

- Built electronic controllers using SCRs for voltage control on viberbowls, electronic SPM meters for press speed, digital decoders for dot matrix displays, and programmable timers for metered lube dispensing.
- Built and installed an automated scrap barrel dumper.
- Installed prototype air flow detector in scrap tube system to detect blockage and automatically shut down presses.

OTHER RELEVANT SKILLS

Skilled in the use of:

oscilloscopes
audio oscillators
signal generators
logic probes
frequency counters

EDUCATION

Diploma, Electrical / Electronic Maintenance
Rothwell Technical Institute, 1997
(2 Year Program)

High School Diploma
Nashville High School, 1995

GEORGE W. BAILOR
503 Wilson Blvd.
New Orleans, LA 12347
Phone: (701) 722-9529
Email: GeoBail@AOL.com

OBJECTIVE

Shipping Leader / Clerk

SUMMARY

Knowledgeable, conscientious Shipping Clerk experienced in the use of rail and truck in the shipment of finished goods throughout the United States. Thorough, accurate, dependable worker with reputation for developing excellent carrier relationships. Good written and verbal communications skills. Noted for being an effective team player.

EXPERIENCE

ATLANTIC FOAM, INC., New Orleans, LA Plant   **1996 to Present**
Major producer of reticulated and un-reticulated polyurethane foam for use in industrial and military applications.

Shipping Leader (2001 – Present)
Reports to Warehouse Supervisor of this 300-employee plant, with responsibility for shipment of finished polyurethane buns to customer accounts throughout the U.S. via truck and rail carriers.

- Receives computerized shipping orders from Operations Manager, including product code, volume, customer name, ship-to address, required delivery date, and transportation mode.
- Arranges orders based upon inventory availability and required delivery date.
- Plans and schedules daily shipments and selects best carriers.
- Contacts carrier dispatchers, ordering needed trucks and/or boxcars and emails copy of bill of lading to same reflecting product classification, volume, and weights.
- Oversees the cleaning of boxcars and trucks to ensure cleanliness and further ensure that finished product arrives in appropriate condition.
- Types and prepares final bills of lading, furnishing warehouse workers with same.
- Prepares and issues loading diagrams and special instructions as needed.
- Oversees the loading of trucks and boxcars, checking for accuracy of shipment and proper loading.
- On military shipments, checks to ensure that product labeling, coding, and packaging conforms to required government specifications.
- Applies door seals to completed orders, and records seal numbers on bill of lading.
- Ensures that driver signs bill of lading acknowledging receipt of load.
- Enters shipping date and carrier information into the computer, completing the final bill of lading and releasing it to Accounts Payable and automatically updating finished goods inventory.
- Tracks and expedites late and/or lost shipments.
- Assists Warehouse Supervisor in conducting weekly and monthly finished goods inventory.
- Helps resolve inventory discrepancies.
- Handles shipment of miscellaneous items as instructed by Warehouse Supervisor.

George W. Bailor   **Page 2**

Zapper Operator (1996 - 2001)
Reported to Shift Supervisor with responsibility for operating the zapper, a steel chamber using a controlled explosion process to remove the cell membranes from un-reticulated foam producing a reticulated (i.e., open pore) polyurethane foam product.

- Loaded mattress-sized un-reticulated polyurethane foam "buns" into the zapper.
- Operated controls, pumping in an explosive mixture of hydrogen and oxygen to required volumes and pressures.
- Depressed the ignite button causing controlled explosion.
- Ran the exhaust and vacuum cycle to discharge burned gasses and product residue.
- Opened zapper chamber, removing and inspecting buns against quality standards.
- Loaded finished product onto conveyor for transport to slitting operations or warehouse storage.
- Checked outside storage tanks gages to ensure ample supply of gasses to support manufacturing requirements.
- Continuously checked tanks and lines to ensure that safe operating conditions were maintained at all times.

EDUCATION

High School Diploma
New Orleans High School, 1996

RELEVANT SKILLS

Use of computer-automated shipping and inventory control systems.
Knowledge of carriers, routes, and rates.
Design / preparation of loading diagrams for efficient rail & truck shipments.
Preparation of bills of lading and standard shipping documents.
Expediting late or lost shipments.
Inventory audit and control procedures.
Certified forklift truck operator.
Use of hand trucks and a variety of small hand tools.

CAROLYN C. FOSTER
92 Sentinel Way
Framingham, MA 23049
Phone: (612) 855-4879
Email: CarFo92l@AOL.com

OBJECTIVE

Shipping Clerk

SUMMARY

Thorough, conscientious, and efficient Shipping Clerk with strong work ethic and reputation for speed and high level of accuracy. Skilled at preparing bills of lading and related shipping documents. Good communication and interpersonal skills. Excellent expeditor of late and/or lost shipments.

EXPERIENCE

CORTLAND MANUFACTURING, INC., Framingham, MA Plant   **1998 to Present**
A 500-employee manufacturer of small electrical household tools and appliances shipped to distributors and retail customers throughout the northeastern United States.

Shipping Clerk (2002 – Present)
Reports to Shipping Supervisor of this electrical appliance manufacturing plant, with responsibility for providing clerical support in the shipment of finished product to customer accounts throughout the northeastern U.S.

- Receives computerized shipping orders from Sales Department.
- Prepares initial bills of lading to reflect customer name, ship-to address, bill-to address, product code, product name, quantities, and base pricing.
- Consults Shipping Supervisor for carrier name and shipping date.
- Releases warehouse copy for use by warehouse workers in the staging of product for shipment purposes.
- Provides Warehouse Supervisor with copies of bill of lading and shipping instructions for use in supervising the loading of trucks and verification of shipment accuracy.
- Issues and records door seals on final bill of lading to ensure security of shipment.
- Ensures signature of truck driver verifying pick-up.
- Records shipping date and releases final bill of lading for distribution to Accounts Payable, Accounts Receivable, and Sales Departments.
- Expedites and tracks rush shipments as requested by Shipping Supervisor.
- Tracks and expedites late and lost shipments as required.
- Assists Shipping Supervisor and Warehouse Manager in conducting physical inventory on a weekly, monthly, and yearly basis.

Accounts Payable Clerk (1998 – 2002)
Reported to Plant Accountant with responsibility for providing clerical support to the Accounts Payable function.

- Compared purchase orders with Receiving Department documentation to verify accuracy of vendor invoices.

- Identified errors, contacting vendors to resolve discrepancies and receive billing adjustments and credit entries.
- Compared bills of lading to carrier invoices, ensuring accuracy and requesting adjustments where appropriate.
- Approved and processed vendor invoices for timely payment, to ensure application of appropriate discounts.
- Researched and handled vendor payment inquiries.
- Negotiated adjustments and/or refunds for damaged and missing goods.
- Maintained accurate, up-to-date records and files.

EDUCATION

High School Diploma
Wilbraham High School, 1998

RELEVANT SKILLS

Typing 65 wpm with high accuracy.
Computer Software –
MS Word
MS Excel
MS Access
SAP

KAREN A. DIERDORF
82 Lincoln Drive
Charlotte, NC 12133
Phone: (615) 772-9801
Email: KarDier@AOL.com

OBJECTIVE

Warehouse Worker – Vital Supplies Delivery

SUMMARY

Skilled forklift truck operator and automated warehouse worker with experience in the prompt and accurate delivery of raw materials and vital supplies to manufacturing units. Hard working, conscientious worker with good communications and interpersonal skills.

EXPERIENCE

REGAL PAPER COMPANY, INC., Charlotte, NC   **2003 to Present**
A 630-employee manufacturing plant producing sanitary consumer paper products for sale though private label distributors and retail outlets.

Warehouse Worker – Vital Supplies Delivery
Report to Warehouse Shift Manager with responsibility for delivering vital supplies and packaging materials to Finishing Department manufacturing units.

- Drives forklift truck in the delivery of palletized packaging materials and vital supplies to Finishing Department production units.
- Continually inventories production units' on-floor inventory supply levels of tail glue, paper cores, poly-wrap, and corrugated knockdown cartons to determine and anticipate delivery needs.
- Juggles delivery schedule to ensure timely delivery of supplies, avoiding shutdowns and costly machine downtime.
- Uses wireless electronic transmitter to track and record inventory withdrawals and deliveries.
- Inputs delivery time, finishing unit number, product name, code, volume and control numbers, thereby maintaining accurate and up-to-date warehouse inventory count.
- Performs end-of-shift physical inventory count of remaining vital supplies and reconciles count with beginning-of-shift inventory levels and on-shift deliveries.
- Ensures that warehouse inventories of vital supplies remain at planned levels to avoid out-of-stock emergencies resulting in machine downtime.
- Immediately notifies Shift Manager whenever inventory levels fall to reorder level, without adequate replenishment.
- Returns out-of-specification materials from finishing unit to warehouse "reclaim area" for return shipment to vendor.
- Ensures the safe and careful operation of forklift vehicle at all times.
- Performs routine safety check of vehicle in accordance with established procedures.

TAYLOR SOUP COMPANY, INC., Lowell, MA Distribution Center   **1992 – 2003**
Major distribution center proving delivery of canned soup products to food distributors and large retail food chain warehouses throughout the northeastern United States.

Forklift Operator
Reported to Distribution Center Shift Supervisor, with responsibility for operation of a forklift truck in the receipt, warehousing, storage, and shipment of palletized loads of canned soup products.

- Used forklift truck to unload incoming trucks and place palletized product on central conveyor for coding, inventorying, and warehousing.
- Operated forklift to remove coded product from central conveyor and deliver to appropriate warehouse storage area.
- Loaded outgoing product shipments into designated trucks and railroad boxcars for shipment to customers.
- Served on warehouse layout taskforce charged with the responsibility to design better product storage patterns aimed at reducing product handling and labor costs.
- Co-chaired Distribution Center safety committee for two years.

EDUCATION

High School Diploma
Portland High School, 1992

COMPANY TRAINING

Forklift Truck Operation
Inventory & Stock Control Using Wireless Technology
OSHA Compliance Seminar
Safety Leadership

JAMES R. SAMUELS

24 River Street
Akron, OH 13231
Phone: (502) 966-1137
Email: JamSaml@AOL.com

OBJECTIVE

Car Loader - Shipping

SUMMARY

Hard-working, conscientious warehouse and distribution worker with 3 years experience as a Car Loader in the Shipping Department of a major tire manufacturer. Skilled in the use of forklift trucks, hand trucks and small hand tools.

EXPERIENCE

HEARTLAND TIRE COMPANY, INC., Akron, OH Plant   **2002 to Present**
A 1,500-employee manufacturing plant engaged in the manufacture of automobile and truck tires.

Car Loader - Shipping
Reports to Shipping Supervisor of this leading tire manufacturer, with responsibility for loading finished product on railroad cars and trucks for shipment to distributors and retail outlets

- Receives shipping orders from Shipping Supervisor.
- Sweeps and vacuums railroad boxcars in preparation for loading product.
- Uses forklift and hand truck to transport required product from warehouse storage to shipment staging area.
- Checks staged product against shipping order to ensure accuracy of shipment with regard to product name, product code and volume.
- Uses forklift and hand truck to load product onto boxcars, following prescribed loading diagram.
- Closes and seals boxcar doors.
- Guides incoming trucks, making sure of proper alignment with loading dock.
- Ensures trucks are properly secured for loading using wheel chucks.
- Sweeps and cleans trucks to ensure cleanliness and appearance.
- Loads trucks in accordance with prescribed loading diagram.
- Checks finished load against bill of lading to ensure accuracy of shipment.
- Affixes door seals to truck doors to ensure security of load.
- Acquires trucker's signature on bill of lading, acknowledging receipt of load.
- Delivers signed bill of lading to Shipping Clerk for billing and accounting purposes.

EDUCATION & TRAINING

High School Diploma
Akron High School

Certified Forklift Driver
Safety at Work Seminar

LINDA E. LINCOLN

25 Tanner Mill Road
East Lansing, MI 16329
Phone: (514) 996-2137
Email: LinLin25@AOL.com

OBJECTIVE

Receiving Clerk

SUMMARY

Energetic, hard-working Receiving Clerk who enjoys working in a busy, high volume Receiving Department. Skilled forklift truck operator noted for accuracy and efficiency in overseeing the receipt, transport, and storage of equipment, raw material, and vital supplies in a fast-paced manufacturing environment. Good math, communications, and team-based skills.

EXPERIENCE

FLEGAL MANUFACTURING, INC., East Lansing Plant　　　　　**2003 to Present**
A 650-employee manufacturing plant producing specialty valves, fittings, and plumbing supplies for shipment to plumbing supply distributors and large retail outlets.

Receiving Clerk
Report to Shipping & Receiving Supervisor of this nationally known plumbing supplies manufacturer. Responsible for the receipt, transport, and storage of all shipments received by the plant including equipment, raw materials, vital supplies, office supplies, etc.

- Receives, directs, and aligns trucks and delivery vehicles with loading dock.
- Ensures trucks and delivery vehicles are secured and safe before unloading.
- Uses forklift truck and hand truck to unload shipment onto loading dock.
- Inventories shipment against packing list and filed copies of purchase order, properly noting any discrepancies.
- Signs driver's documentation, acknowledging delivery and receipt of shipment.
- Signs purchase order, acknowledging receipt.
- Attaches packing list and bill of lading to purchase order, delivering completed paperwork to Shipping & Receiving Supervisor.
- Transports and stores equipment, raw materials, and vital supplies in designated warehouse storage area and enters data into computerized inventory system.
- Hand delivers miscellaneous shipments to originator of purchase order, securing appropriate signature acknowledging delivery and receipt.
- Assists Shipping & Receiving Supervisor in performing weekly and monthly physical inventory count and audits.

WARFIELD SECURITY COMPANY, INC., Detroit, MI　　　　　**1992 – 2003**
Contract security firm providing guards, alarm systems, and complete security systems to manufacturing and retail companies.

Truck Driver (1997 – 2003)
Reported to Distribution Center Manager, with responsibility for delivering security alarms and protective equipment to customer job sites.

Linda E. Lincoln   **Page 2**

- Used order pick list to fill customer orders from inventory stock.
- Checked accuracy of order against customer's purchase order.
- Prepared packing list, accurately reflecting shipment.
- Loaded truck and made delivery to customer's site.
- Delivered equipment, and secured customer signature acknowledging receipt.
- Returned packing list and signed receipt to Distribution Center Manager.

Security Guard (1992 – 1997)
Reported to Night Security Manager, providing 3rd shift guard security services at various manufacturing and retail stores throughout the Detroit area.

EDUCATION

High School Diploma
East Lansing High School, 1992

SKILLS & TRAINING

Certified Forklift and Electric Hand Truck Operator
Good Math and Written Communication Skills
Safe Operating Practices Seminar

JOANNE L. SIMINGTON
211 Ocean Breeze Way
Santa Barbara, CA 12847

Home: (949) 664-8937   Email: JoSimi@MSN.com   Cell: (949) 746-8273

OBJECTIVE

Warehouse Worker

SUMMARY

Hardworking, dependable Warehouse Worker / Forklift Operator with experience working in modern, computerized warehousing operation. Efficient, motivated individual with reputation for thoroughness and accuracy. Team player with good communication and interpersonal skills.

EXPERIENCE

WESTCO PRODUCTS, INC., Santa Barbara Plant   **2003 to Present**
Leading manufacturer of video games and electronic consumer entertainment products.

Warehouse Worker
Report to Warehouse Supervisor with responsibility for operation of a forklift truck in the receiving storage and in-plant delivery of raw materials and supplies.

- Operate forklift trucks and specialized material / pallet handling equipment.
- Operate ground swing-reach and "man-up swing-reach" to receive and store pallets from rack locations and warehouse staging locations and delivery to production line operations.
- Move and maintain accurate inventory of packaging materials and vital supplies.
- Assist in training of warehouse employees in the operation of forklift trucks and swing-reach equipment.
- Load and unload trailers; transport tool truck and trash bins.
- Locate and store materials in rack storage.
- Order supplies from warehouse using computerized pick-list.
- Maintain returned goods inventory.

WARSAW INSTRUMENT COMPANY, Los Angeles, CA   **1998 - 2003**
A quality leader in the manufacture of magnetic and liquid flow calibration meters.

Department Clerk / Material Handler
Reported to Shipping and Receiving Supervisor with responsibility for performing various clerical support functions in support of receiving operations.

- Performed clerical functions using computerized printouts and documents.
- Operated card-sorting machines and card readers when receiving machine parts.
- Used personal computer to look up reference status of parts sent and/or received.

- Maintained inventory of parts for accountability and record keeping.

EDUCATION

High School Diploma
Pasadena High School, 1998

COMPANY TRAINING

Warehouse Computer Inventory System
Swing-reach Equipment Operation
Forklift Truck Operation
Safe Work Practices
Total Quality

MICHAEL J. WILLINGHAM
825-B Walter Reed Parkway
Washington, DC 23846

Home: (218) 946-3850   Email: MichWil825@AOL.com   Cell: (214) 772-9824

OBJECTIVE

Laboratory Technician – Quality Control

SUMMARY

Over eight years experience as a Senior Quality Control Lab Technician and Lab Technician in the polymer chemicals industry. Skilled in the use of a wide range of testing and laboratory techniques to ensure adherence to in-process and finished product quality standards. Enjoy solid reputation for accuracy, reliability, and efficiency. Good communication and interpersonal skills.

EXPERIENCE

PIPER POLYMER SPECIALTIES, INC., Alexandria, VA   **1996 to Present**
The Alexandria plant employs 350 employees and produces specialty chemicals, including TDI and resins, for use in the manufacture of polyurethane foams and other polymer-based products.

Senior Lab Technician – Quality Control (2004 - Present)
Report to Laboratory Supervisor with responsibility for providing a variety of tests to ensure that finished products meet required quality and safety standards.

- Utilize AA, Laser Particle Sizer, FTIR, GC, and HPLC to perform a variety of quality tests following prescribed procedures and protocols.
- Maintain and troubleshoot instruments, arranging for service and repair as needed.
- Assist in executing IQ/OQ protocols and reports for new equipment.
- Assist in performing method and instrument verifications.
- Consult with Laboratory Supervisor on method, specification, and testing problems.
- Train new Technicians on laboratory and safety procedures.
- Maintain accurate records and reports on testing results.
- Work closely with plant operating personnel to remedy out-of-specification quality issues.
- Maintain in-house hazardous materials management system.
- Assist in training operating personnel in the safe handling and disposal of chemical materials.
- Serve as a member of the plant safety committee.

Laboratory Technician – Quality Control (1996 – 2004)
Reported to Senior Lab Technician with responsibility for providing a variety of tests to ensure compliance with required product quality standards.

- Collected and analyzed in-process and finished product samples for testing.
- Performed required test procedures following prescribed protocols.
- Recorded and maintained accurate records of test results.

Michael J. Willingham **Page 2**

- Reported out-of-specification issues to Senior Lab Technician for resolution.
- Assisted in the troubleshooting and repair of lab instruments.
- Monitored and analyzed materials handling records and documentation to spot and report noncompliance issues to lab management for resolution with operating personnel.

EDUCATION

High School Diploma
Wilson High School, 1996

COMPANY TRAINING

Instrumental Techniques
Quality Control Testing
Statistical Process Control
Hazardous Materials Handling
Safe Practices
Microsoft Excel

WILMA D. DAVIDSON
915 Grey Fox Road
Louisville, KY 23130
Phone: (912) 695-4782
Email: WilDD@AOL.com

OBJECTIVE

Quality Control Technician / Specialist

SUMMARY

Thorough, conscientious Quality Control Technician / Specialist with 7 years experience in a pharmaceutical manufacturing and packaging operation. Solid laboratory and testing skills combined with online quality measuring and control. Skilled at relating out-of-specification process causes to product quality issues and working closely with Operations personnel in implementing remedial action designed to rapidly return product to required standards. Excellent communication, conflict management, and interpersonal skills.

EXPERIENCE

BIOPHASE PARMA GROUP, INC. Louisville, KY Plant   **1993 to Present**
A leading manufacturer of over-the-counter drugs and remedies including antacids, cold remedies, analgesics, and antihistamine products.

Quality Control Technician (1997 to Present)
Report to Manager of Quality Control with responsibility for continuously monitoring the quality and efficacy of products to ensure they meet and/or exceed company quality standards and comply with government regulations.

- Collect in-process samples and perform various laboratory tests to ensure products conform to required quality standards and government regulations.
- Oversee online testing to ensure proper protocol and use of acceptable procedures.
- Assist line operating personnel in troubleshooting quality variances, identifying causes, and taking prompt remedial action to reduce unnecessary waste through product rejection.
- Maintain complete and accurate records and reports.
- Train new line operators in proper quality sampling and testing procedures.
- Exercise critical decision-making skills in shutting line down due to malfunctioning equipment, preventing rework and unnecessary operating expense.
- Record and monitor weights and codes of finished product.

Line Operator - Packaging (1994 – 1997)
Reported to Packaging Supervisor with responsibility for efficiently running a high-speed packaging line and achieving both production and quality standards.

- Operated high-speed packaging equipment to include performance of mechanical adjustments for product changeovers, quality assurance monitoring, label review, and input of required data into Operations computer system.

Wilma D. Davidson   **Page 2**

- Performed Total Productive Maintenance, learning progressive maintenance skills including basic mechanical troubleshooting.
- Adhered to job hazard analysis and safe practice procedures, completing behavioral observation surveys to prevent injuries.
- Participated as a member of the Plant Safe Practices Team.

Production Scheduling Clerk (1993 – 1994)
Reported to Production Scheduler with responsibility for inputting machine loading data into computerized production schedule, and releasing finalized packaging line production schedules to Operations Manager.

EDUCATION

High School Diploma
Louisville Central High School, 1993

COMPANY TRAINING

Quality Control Testing
Total Quality
Forklift Truck Operation
Compounding
Safety Leadership
Basic Hand Tools
Basic Mechanics
Computer Basics

JOAN A. LIEBERMAN
1324 Overview Road
Cleveland, OH 13295

Home: (214) 775-2847   Email: DorrLieb@MSN.com   Office: (214) 772-9824

OBJECTIVE

Laboratory Technician – Chemical or Personal Products Industries

SUMMARY

Over six years experience as a Lab Technician in the pharmaceutical industry. Skilled in the use of a variety of testing and laboratory techniques in the areas of microbiology and quality assurance involving compliance, identification of organisms, media preparation, and lab documentation. Noted for being efficient, conscientious, thorough, and highly accurate.

EXPERIENCE

BIER PRODUCTS, INC., Sandusky, OH   **1999 to Present**
The Sandusky plant employs 350 employees and manufactures private label personal products such as toothpaste, shampoos, hand lotions, and some over-the-counter cold remedies.

Lab Technician – Microbiology
Report to Laboratory Supervisor with responsibility for providing a variety of tests to ensure quality, compliance, and safety of products.

- Perform validation of cleaning and sanitizing procedures to ensure government compliance.
- Test and approve finished products, stability, raw materials, and de-ionized water using aseptic sampling techniques and compendial microbiological methods.
- Collect information for investigation and resolution of out-of-specification results and identified unknown organisms.
- Use autoclave for media preparation and sterilization of equipment.
- Maintain aseptic, sanitary environment for microbiology lab "clean room".
- Coordinate corporate GMP and SOP compliance audits with appropriate follow-up to assure further adherence to standards.
- Manage expiration and label control of all reagents and media; maintaining lab documentation audit system.
- Serve as member of sensory evaluation panel responsible for organoleptic approval of consumer products.
- Serve as trainer in instructing compounding personnel in proper aseptic water collection techniques.
- Devised more effective record keeping system, allowing faster retrieval of records.
- Introduced initialing system to eliminate documentation and testing errors.

Joan A. Lieberman   **Page 2**

WALTON PAPER COMPANY, Toledo, OH   **1996 –1999**
The Toledo plant manufactures a full range of consumer paper products including toilet tissue, facial tissue, and towels under the brand name of Softie. The plant employs 400 workers.

Lab Technician – Quality Laboratory
Reported to Quality Control Supervisor with responsibility for running a variety of tests to ensure that all products manufactured conformed to plant quality standards.

- Collected samples of both in-process and finished products for testing purposes.
- Performed various laboratory tests for tensile strength, absorbency, wet strength, and hand feel.
- Provided rapid feedback to operating personnel on out-of-specification product.
- Tested packaging materials (poly wraps and corrugated) to ensure vendor compliance with required packaging material standards.

EDUCATION

High School Diploma
Sandusky High School, 1996

University of Toledo
Courses in Biology and Organic Chemistry
2000 and 2001

COMPANY TRAINING

Microsoft Windows
Microsoft Word for Windows
Microsoft Excel
Manufacturing Practices

GEORGE P. MASON
126-A South Street
Philadelphia, PA 19355

Home: (215) 557-9682   Email: GeoMa126@AOL.com   Office: (215) 457-9328

OBJECTIVE

Medical / Biochemical Research Technician

SUMMARY

Skilled Medical / Biochemical Research Technician with more than 8 years production and reagent manufacture, thyroid & neuroendocrine, and reproductive endocrine laboratory and clinical research experience. Conscientious, dedicated, and methodical laboratory worker with solid academic training and reputation for thoroughness and accuracy. Excellent written communication skills.

EXPERIENCE

BIO REAGENTS, INC., Philadelphia, PA   **2002 to Present**
A leading laboratory and manufacturer / supplier of biochemical reagents.

Senior Research Technician
Report to Chief Research Scientist – Reagent R&D with the following responsibilities:

- Develop immunoassays (total t3, estradiol, digoxin, LH, PSA, etc.).
- Supervise Hapten technical support group.
- Perform clinical evaluations, stability studies, and 510K protocols.
- Establish control specifications and write SOPs.

HOSPITAL OF THE UNIVERSITY OF PENNSYLVANIA, Philadelphia, PA   **1997 – 2002**

Research Technician – Thyroid & Neuroendocrine Laboratory (1999 - 2002)
Reported to Medical Research Scientist in support of basic research and clinical studies.

- In-vitro studies (regulation of pituitary glycoprotein hormone production by hypothalmic factors in human pituitary adenomas).
- Clinical studies (effect of hyperprolactinemia & hypogonadism on bone mass and the effects of hypothalamic regulatory factors in patients with pituitary adenomas).
- Tissue culture, DNA/RNA analysis; protein biochemistry & radioimmunoassay.

Research Technician – Reproductive Endocrine Laboratory (1997 – 1999)
Reported to Medical Research Scientist in support of basic and clinical research studies.

- Provided laboratory support in studies of nutritional effects on reproductive endocrinology.
- Utilized total parental nutritional model (employing surgical implantation of cannulae, blood sampling, radioimmunoassay, etc.).

EDUCATION

A.S. Degree – Biotechnology
Weidner University, 1997

High School Diploma
Henderson High School, 1995

TRAINING WORKSHOPS & SEMINARS

Design of Experiments
Instrumental Analysis
Research Protocol
Statistical Process Control
Project Management
Statistical Data Exploration

COMPUTER SKILLS

JMP Statistical
Windows 2000 & Me
FileMaker Pro
Microsoft Office Suite

PROFESSIONAL AFFILIATIONS

ASQ
AACC
CLAS

CARLOS B. RODRIQUEZ
133 5th Street
Reading, PA 19328

Home: (610) 522-6439   Email: CarRodz@AOL.com   Cell: (610) 553-9048

OBJECTIVE

Environmental Specialist - Manufacturing

SUMMARY

Skilled Environmental Specialist with extensive experience in compliance with federal and state governmental environmental regulations including SuperFund Amendment Reauthorization Act (SARA), Resource Conservation and Recovery Act (RCRA), Clean Air Act (CAA), and Clean Water Act (CWA). Conscientious, motivated self-starter noted for bringing continuous improvement to operations.

EXPERIENCE

HARRINGTON PRODUCTS INC., Reading, PA Plant   **1993 to Present**
The Harrington plant is a 375-employee, team-based manufacturing plant that produces over-the-counter pharmaceuticals, including cold remedies, cough syrups, and antihistamine products.

Site Environmental Specialist (2001 to Present)
Report to Plant Engineering Manager with responsibility for maintaining and improving all plant environmental systems to ensure full compliance with local, state, and federal environmental regulations.

- Write SARA 313 Form R Report, 312 Tier II Report, Waste Energy and Cost Report, all internal and external environmental reports, and monthly sewer discharge report for local sewer authority.
- Serve as plant liaison with Environmental Protection Agency, Department of Environmental Protection, publicly-owned treatment works, and local fire department.
- Achieved 98% environmental rating during corporate audit (highest rating in company history).
- Received State award and cited as model plant for manufacturing environmental systems.
- Conducted bi-annual RCRA training for entire plant.
- Coordinated entire permit application process to construct bag houses for jet milling system, achieving approval by Pennsylvania DEP.
- Generated cost savings of approximately $70,000 on Title V application submittal.
- Track all waste streams on MS Excel program.
- Coordinate compliance emissions testing for thermal oxidizer and particulate bag houses.
- Maintain computerized MSDS system and training for Terms Environmental Regulations Compliance Program.

Compounding Technician (1998 – 2001)
Reported to Shift Operations Supervisor with responsibility for operating and maintaining a product compounding operation.

Carlos B. Rodriquez

- Operated and maintained batch mixing process, drum dryers, thermal oxidizer, bag houses, and air jet milling equipment.
- Operated and maintained all pumps, scales, HPI computer system, control room equipment, and mobile powder dump station.
- Performed analytical work involved in monitoring Benzene removal system.
- Continuously monitored all steam and air pressures, and performed preventive maintenance on all equipment.

Product QC Technician   (1994 – 1998)
Shipping Clerk   (1993 – 1994)

EDUCATION

High School Diploma
Wilson High School, 1992

COMPANY TRAINING

Spill Response Program
Fire Response Training
Corporate Environmental Certification
Handling & Disposal of Hazardous Substances
Safety Leadership

COMPUTER SKILLS

Honeywell TDC 3000 Control Systems

DAVID T. BENSON
126 North Willow Road.
Wilmington, DE 19284

Home: (305) 997-2938   Email: DavBen@AOL.com   Cell: (305) 989-2205

OBJECTIVE

Accounting – Accounts Payable or Finished Goods Inventory Clerk

SUMMARY

Over ten years plant accounting and administrative support with a leading manufacturer of consumer products. Strengths include excellent communication skills, high level of accuracy, and strong work ethic. Team player noted for ability to work independently with little guidance and direction. Highly dependable, thorough, and efficient.

EXPERIENCE

TYSON CONSUMER PRODUCTS, INC., Wilmington, DE Plant   **1994 to Present**
Major plant site employing 1,200 employees and engaged in the manufacture of shampoos, hair products, hand soaps, and other personal care products.

Accounting Clerk – Accounts Payable / Finished Goods (2003 – Present)
Report to Senior Manufacturing Cost Accountant with responsibility for providing accounting and administrative support in the areas of accounts payable, and raw materials / finished products inventory accounting.
- Tracked daily raw materials receipts, reconciling them with vendor invoices and approving payment.
- Monitored daily inventory activity and adjustments for plant site and 15 contracts sites.
- Interfaced with vendor community, Production Planning & Receiving personnel on accounting and inventory issues.
- Oversaw daily operation of automatic finished goods inventory system. Reconciled daily reports used to track production, shipments, and movement of finished goods.
- Analyzed end-of-month inventory reports to ensure correct quantities of finished goods were passed on to the cost accounting system.
- Worked with plant and contract personnel to perform physical inventory audits.
- Compiled end-of-month reports, showing "total delivered cost" using Microsoft Excel.
- Developed procedures and forms for use in monitoring "miscellaneous shipments" from plant.
- Instructed and trained plant personnel in use of new "Order for Shipment" procedures, resulting in better audit control of company assets.

Payroll Clerk (1999 – 2003)
Reported to Manager of Compensation and Benefits with responsibility for all clerical support functions in support of the plant's payroll system.
- Tracked attendance, printed checks, and reconciled payroll check numbers.
- Made adjustments to errors on previous week's timesheets and prepared hand-typed checks.
- Initiated Federal Reserve checks for Savings Bonds and requests for vacation pay advances.
- Analyzed overtime, calculated average pay for Workmen's Compensation and disability cases, and supplied information to Disability Review Board.

DAVID T. BENSON   **Page 2**

Inventory Control Clerk (1994 – 1999)
Reported to Inventory Control Manager with responsibility for maintaining appropriate levels of raw material inventories to support plant manufacturing operations.
- Tracked raw material and packaging inventory levels to ensure availability and accuracy.
- Maintained adequate levels of inventory to support production needs.
- Assisted in determining adequate raw material and packing supply inventory levels required to support manufacture of new products.

EDUCATION

High School Diploma
Wilmington High School, 1994

COMPANY TRAINING

Microsoft Windows
Microsoft Excel
MRP, ASI, MCAC, FPI

DONNA A. JACKSON
214 Meadow Road
Denver, CO 21948

Home: (602) 844-9039   Email: DonJck@MSN.com   Cell: (602) 355-9987

OBJECTIVE

Accounting Clerk or Administrative Support Position in Manufacturing Environment

SUMMARY

Conscientious, motivated worker with over six years accounting support experience in a manufacturing environment. Skilled in accounts payable and cash management. Known for being a solid team player with the ability to work independently and accurately with little or no supervision.

EXPERIENCE

KENNSINGTON COMPANY, Denver, CO Plant   **1999 to Present**
Manufacturer of consumer paper products and packing materials. Plant employs 275 employees and houses manufacturing, warehousing and shipping operations, supplying paper and packaging material distributors throughout the Midwest and Rocky Mountain states.

Accounts Payable Clerk (2003 – Present)
Report to Senior Accountant with responsibility for providing clerical and administrative support services in connection with the Accounts Payable function.
- Responsible for audit and prompt payment of all accounts payable invoices.
- Process over 20,000 invoices annually, with high degree of efficiency and accuracy.
- Interface with vendor community and corporate management in resolving payable issues.
- Process monthly journal entries and reconcile monthly balance sheet accounts.
- Act as Administrative Assistant to Plant Accounting Department.
- Coordinate and arrange for various business meetings and functions.
- Alternate with Payroll Clerk, with responsibility for computing work hours, running checks, and updating the corporate payroll system.
- Reconcile plant payroll.

Plant Cashier (1999 – 2003)
Report to Accounting Manager with responsibility for daily management of the plant's petty cash account.
- Maintained and accounted for $7,000 petty cash fund.
- Monthly reconciled cash account.
- Made bank deposits.
- Provided clerical assistance to Payroll and Accounts Payable functions.

EDUCATION

High School Diploma
East Denver High School, 1999

MARY ANN KESSLER
832 Ocean Drive, West
Ocean Park, CA 28394

Home: (949) 882-9785   Email: MaKes@AOL.com   Cell: (949) 884-2738

OBJECTIVE

Computer Technician/Lead Technician in Manufacturing Plant

SUMMARY

Extensive experience in computer troubleshooting and data collection/analysis in a plant manufacturing setting. Skilled at using database decision-making in the design and/or improvement of various operations and systems. Broad-based PC skills including hardware, software, troubleshooting, and maintenance skills for multi-computer networks. Hands-on experience in Operations, Warehousing, and Logistics complements strong PC-related competencies.

EXPERIENCE

HAMPFILL PAPER COMPANY, INC., Irving, CA Plant   **1998 to Present**
Flagship manufacturing site of this $800 million paper specialties manufacturer. Plant employs 1,500 employees with daily manufacturing capacity of 450 tons.

Lead Technician – Process Reliability (2003 – Present)
Report to Manager of Quality Reliability with responsibility for tracking and monitoring process reliability data for paper manufacturing processes.
- Provide centralized tracking and reporting of efficiency and process reliability data for 10 separate manufacturing operations. (Collected data from dedicated production PCs.)
- Collect and analyze individual operation production tracking reports, presenting results to both department and plant leadership.
- Led software changeover to Microsoft for use in production tracking.
- Serve as technical support for Plant's use of Microsoft Quality Windows software, contributing to 14 consecutive months of above-average process reliability results.
- Provide maintenance and troubleshooting support for 21 Operations PCs.

Logistics Planning Coordinator   (1998 – 2003)
Reported to Logistics Planning Manager with responsibility for coordinating the ordering and maintenance of raw materials and packaging inventories in support of Plant manufacturing schedule.
- Ordered and expedited delivery of packaging supplies and raw materials to supply Plant manufacturing operations based upon sales forecast and manufacturing schedule.
- Developed and implemented Cycle Count Program for planning raw materials delivery.
- Validated new Materials Requirements Planning System (MRP) for tissue products.
- Expedited finished goods approval and shipment.
- Used word processing, spreadsheets, graphs, and MRP software for planning purposes.
- Served as PC troubleshooting resource for Plant operations.

MARY ANN KESSLER   **Page 2**

WALTON PRODUCTS, INC., Bristol, CT Plant   **1992 – 1998**
Manufacturing plant employing 235 workers engaged in the manufacture and distribution of a wide range
of cleaning supplies and chemicals for commercial and industrial applications.

Leader – Warehouse & Receiving (1994 – 1998)
Led team of seven workers responsible for receiving, storage, and delivery of over 400 supply items to
manufacturing operations.
- Streamlined receiving operations, resulting in elimination of overtime and reduction of average
  turnaround time from 5 days to 1.5 days.
- Initiated new warehouse storage design, increasing warehouse storage capacity by 25%.
- Designed and implemented new procedures to complement short-cycle inventories and high-
  performing work system.

Returns Inspector (1992 – 1994)
Responsible for the inspection, evaluation, and processing of product returns.
- Initiated procedures for rework process, reducing rework contractor expense by $25,000
  annually.
- Assisted in the design and layout of rework process area for processing product returns.

EDUCATION

High School Diploma
Bristol High School, 1992

COMPUTER SKILLS

DOS	Windows	Excel
Word for Windows	PowerPoint	MS Project
Lotus	Harvard Graphics	WordPerfect
Print Shop	Instant Artist	PC Maintenance
PC Troubleshooting	MRP Systems	

COMPANY TRAINING

Quality Assurance	Statistical Analysis	Total Quality
DOT Hazardous Materials	Safety Leadership	Fork Lift Operation
Short-Cycle Management	Lean Manufacturing	Critical Thinking

WANDA J. COOPER
8632 Washington Street
Detroit, MI 13295

Home: (313) 372-5598   Email: Wancoo@AOL.com   Cell: (313) 669-3340

OBJECTIVE

Senior Information Systems Technician or Administrator – Manufacturing / Quality

SUMMARY

Highly skilled, conscientious Information Systems Administrator with experience in technical support, quality assurance, inventory management, product development, production and warehouse operations. Strong technical and interpersonal skills. Extensive work experience in a team-based manufacturing environment.

COMPUTER SKILLS

Software: MS Windows, Word, Excel, PowerPoint, Harvard Graphics, SQC Pack/Plus (statistical), and StarGraphics (statistical)

Hardware: IBM PS/2, AT, XT, HP Vectra ES-12 & ES-16, and Compaq personal computers and compatibles.

EXPERIENCE

CARSON PRODUCTS, INC., Detroit, MI Plant   **1992 to Present**
The Detroit plant is a 525-employee, high-performance work system manufacturing facility producing private label skin moisteners, hand creams, toothpaste, cold remedies, and cough syrups.

PC Support Technician (2003 to Present)
Report to Information Systems Manager with responsibility for providing technical support to 25 department microprocessor users.

- Provides microprocessor hardware and software installation support, including connectivity to plant network system configuration and expansion.
- Assists Management Systems Department in conducting NetCensus and security audits.
- Handles system maintenance, upgrades, and repairs in support of department needs.
- Compiles documentation of system hardware and software for plant asset tracking.
- Functions as a resource for application support of MS Office and various other software products.
- Interfaces with outside vendors in providing system repairs, purchases, and new installations.

Compliance Audit Assistant (2001 – 2003)
Reported to Compliance and Audit Manager with responsibility for assisting in the management of control systems in accordance with FDA requirements for computerized drug processing and quality control standards. Ensures integrity of both input and output data.

- Managed analytical quality status control and sequential batch lot numbering for Quality Assurance Department.

Wanda J. Cooper **Page 2**

- Monitored electronic batch record retention for accuracy.
- Audited packaging record documentation and electronic record information.
- Authorized release of finished goods production for customer shipment.
- Prepare monthly statistical product quality reports.
- Generate periodic SARA reports for Environmental Department on hazardous materials as required for compliance with state and federal regulations.
- Evaluate inventory control, variation tracking, and reconciliation of bulk product, raw materials, and packaging for Logistics Department.

Manufacturing Systems Technician (1999 – 2001)
Reported to Manger of Quality Assurance with responsibility for implementation, validation, and quality review of testing practices, documentation, and results for computerized material tracking/quality control system.

- Served as plant-wide gatekeeper and in-house technical expert on data retrieval systems for use across all plant functions.
- Coordinated change control process of FDA original records from hardcopy to electronic retention.
- Maintained security data and assigned security level authorization.
- Performed SQL and minor Pascal-based programming (REXX) for data retrieval.
- Assisted in the development of training manual and standard operating procedure documentation.
- Facilitated classroom training on system use and conducted qualification testing for 200 operations employees.

Pilot Plant Technician (1997 - 1999)
Quality Inspector (1995 – 1997)
Warehouse Worker (1992 – 1995)

EDUCATION

High School Diploma
East Detroit High School, 1992

COMPANY TRAINING

Good Manufacturing Practices for Drug & Medical Devices
FDA Compliance Policy Guidelines for Computerized Drug Testing
Statistical Process Control – Total Quality Management
Business Resource Planning – Short Cycle Management
Computer Systems Training
Hazardous Materials Handling
Leadership Safety Training

CAROL A. DERSTEIN
206 Carter Avenue
Springfield, MA 13295

Home: (602) 422-5183   Email: Carders@AOL.com   Cell: (602) 435-9827

OBJECTIVE

Process Reliability / Systems Technician - Manufacturing

SUMMARY

Technically proficient Process Reliability and Manufacturing Systems Technician with extensive experience in computer troubleshooting, data collection, and analysis in a manufacturing environment. Skilled in the use of databased decision making to design and/or improve manufacturing operations and systems. Broad based PC skills in hardware, software, troubleshooting, and systems maintenance support.

COMPUTER SKILLS

DOS	Windows	Excel	Word for Windows
PowerPoint	MS Project	Lotus	Harvard Graphics
WordPerfect	Print Shop	Instant Artist	MRP Systems
MS Word	Access	PC Maintenance	PC Troubleshooting

EXPERIENCE

HUBER MANUFACTURING, INC., Holyoke, MA Plant   **1993 to Present**
The Holyoke plant is a 400-employee, team-based manufacturing plant that produces over-the-counter pharmaceuticals, lotions, skin creams, and personal hygiene products.

Process Reliability Technician – Manufacturing Systems (2004 to Present)
Report to Manager of Process Reliability with responsibility for centralized tracking and reporting of efficiency and process reliability data for 10 pharmaceutical process manufacturing lines.

- Collect and analyze individual production line production tracking reports, presenting findings to department and Operations management.
- Use MS Excel, PowerPoint, and Word for Windows for tracking and reporting results on a daily basis.
- Serve as plant technical resource for use of Quality Windows software, contributing key training and technical support that resulted in 18 consecutive months of record-breaking process reliability.
- Provide maintenance and troubleshooting support for 10 manufacturing process PC's.
- Instrumental in leading changeover to Microsoft software for process reliability tracking and reporting purposes.

Carol A. Derstein   **Page 2**

Process Returns Leader (2001 – 2004)
Reported to Shift Operations Manager with responsibility for overseeing 32 employees in the efficient and cost effective processing of customer returns and rework of suntan lotion product.

- Handled all issues and problems with regard to staffing, scheduling, operations, budgeting, process improvement, and data tracking.
- Decreased labor costs in both Returns and Rework operations by 35% within 2 seasons through more efficient work processing methods.
- Worked with outside firm to successfully transfer all Returns and Rework on an outsourcing basis with 20% overall cost reduction annually.
- Served as plant technical resource for PC troubleshooting support.

Logistics Planning Associate (1999 – 2001)
Reported to Plant Logistics Manager with responsibility for monitoring, ordering, and expediting delivery of raw materials and packaging supplies to support plant manufacturing operations.

- Forecasted, ordered, and scheduled delivery of raw materials and packaging supplies based on production schedule.
- Developed and implemented cycle count program for packaging and raw materials needs forecasting.
- Validated New Materials Requirements Planning System (MRP) for new skin lotion product manufacturing line.
- Served as plant technical resource, providing PC troubleshooting support services.

Receiving Leader – Warehousing Operations (1996 – 1999)
Forklift Operator – Shipping & Receiving   (1993 – 1996)

EDUCATION

High School Diploma
Holyoke High School, 1993

COMPANY TRAINING

Leading by Leadership	DOT Hazardous Materials
Quality Assurance	Good Manufacturing Practices
Total Quality	Forklift Truck Operation
Short Cycle Management	Compounding
Statistical Analysis	Safety Leadership

TERRANCE B. FOSTER

2245 Cliffside Road
Vancouver, WA 13246

Home: (801) 775-2948   Email: TerraFo@MSN.com   Cell: (801) 339-4076

OBJECTIVE

Microcomputer Support Specialist - Manufacturing

SUMMARY

Knowledgeable, skilled Microcomputer Support Specialist with 12 years experience in microcomputer installation, application, troubleshooting and training in a process manufacturing setting. Strong interpersonal and communications skills. Self-starter noted for responsiveness and strong client support focus. Enjoys working in a team-based, high performance work environment.

COMPUTER SKILLS

MS Windows 3.1	MS Word 2.0	MS Excel 4.0	Lotus 1-2-3
Multimate	Harvard Graphics	NetCensus	Pascal
DOS	PC Troubleshooting	Internal E-Mail	

EXPERIENCE

WALLACE PRODUCTS COMPANY, INC., Vancouver, WA Plant   **1992 to Present**
The Vancouver plant is a 650-employee, team-based manufacturing plant that produces over-the-counter and prescription pharmaceuticals and skin treatment products.

Systems Technician (2003 to Present)
Report to Manager of Process Reliability with responsibility for centralized tracking and reporting of efficiency and process reliability data for 10 pharmaceutical process manufacturing lines.

- Support and troubleshoot the computer inventory tracking and quality control system (HPI) at the user level.
- Manage information for Packaging Department regarding HPI installation and maintenance.
- Perform Pascal-based programming for information retrieval using REXX.
- Developed and ran HPI system training program for line operating personnel.
- Serve as compliance auditor of production documentation for Packaging Department, with responsibility for authorizing release of product.

PC Specialist (2000 – 2003)
Reported to Plant IS Manager with responsibility for providing technical support to 22 manufacturing operating personnel end users in the use of PC's.

- Provided application support for Microsoft Windows, Word 2.0 and Excel 4.0 to PC users.

- Performed microcomputer installation, configuration and expansion including connectivity to Plant network and software installation.
- Performed system upgrades to accommodate department needs and acted as liaison for IS Department.
- Maintained documentation of system hardware and software fir Plant asset tracking and audit.
- Provided interface with outside vendors for PC repairs and purchases.
- Provided software training in a classroom setting and on a one-on-one basis.

Process Safety Engineer   (1997 – 2000)
Machine Operator – Packaging (1992 – 1997)

EDUCATION

High School Diploma
Vancouver High School, 1992

COMPANY TRAINING

Total Quality Management
Statistical Process Control
Good Manufacturing Practices
Short Cycle Management
Leadership Practices

KAREN D. MARSHALL
5001 Brooklawn Blvd.
Birmingham, AL 23195

Home: (512) 244-7953   Email: KarMar@AOL.com   Cell: (512) 364-9827

OBJECTIVE

Human Resources – Benefits Clerk / HR Assistant

SUMMARY

Accurate, efficient, detail-oriented Group Benefits Clerk with broad benefits enrollment, record-keeping, and administrative experience. Strong communications and interpersonal skills combined with the ability to multitask and juggle priorities. Noted for being highly responsive to the needs of both employees and management.

EXPERIENCE

WILSHIRE COMPANY, Birmingham, AL   **2001 to Present**
Leading manufacturer of builders' hardware. Plant employs 2,500 employees and houses manufacturing, warehousing and shipping operations, supplying builders' hardware and hand tools to retail chains throughout the southeastern U.S.

Group Benefits Clerk
Report to Plant Benefits Manager with responsibility for managing all clerical and administrative support functions in the enrollment and ongoing administration of employee benefit programs at this 2,500-employee plant site.

- Enrolls all new employees in group insurance benefits programs, including group health insurance, life insurance, AD&D, and disability coverages.
- Provides new employee benefits orientation presentations, explaining options and answering employee questions with regard to same.
- Ensures that all new employee enrollment forms are properly completed and returned on a timely basis.
- Explains vacation benefits, maternity leave of absence, pay policies, and other relevant Human Resource policies to new hires, as outlined in the Employee Handbook.
- Tracks and processes over 650 employees during annual insurance "open enrollment" period.
- Handles all employee benefit changes (e.g., name changes, address changes, beneficiary changes, changes in coverage limits, etc.).
- Processes short-term disability claims.
- Tracks employees on leaves-of-absence (i.e., medical, short-term disability, maternity leave).
- Prepares and disseminates literature and benefit change forms in connection with standard benefit programs and new program rollouts.
- Counsels and assists employees with claims problems.
- Processes COBRA enrollment on separated employees.
- Prepares various benefits analysis, summaries, and reports as requested.
- Streamlined a number of benefits processes and procedures, saving the company an estimated $40,000 annually in reduced labor costs.

Karen D. Marshall   **Page 2**

BIRMINGHAM SUPPLY COMPANY, Birmingham, AL   **1998 - 2001**
Distributor of copper tubing and plumbing supplies to residential and commercial builders in the Greater Birmingham market.

HR Administrative Assistant
Reported to Controller with responsibility for handling all group benefits programs and other HR-related services for this 60-employee distributor.

- Handled all employee benefits program enrollments and changes.
- Coordinated processing of insurance claims with carriers.
- Counseled employees regarding claims eligibility and claims issues.
- Tracked employee attendance and hours worked.
- Assisted with payroll preparation.
- Handled payroll questions and resolved discrepancies.
- Prepared various analysis and reports as requested.

EDUCATION

High School Diploma
Birmingham High School, 1998

COMPUTER SKILLS

MS Office – Word, Excel, PowerPoint, Access Database
PeopleSoft - HRIS

SANDRA E. BULLOCK
205 North Beacon Road
Providence, RI 29385

Home: (614) 255-2394 | Email: SnBull@AOL.com | Office: (614) 558-9137

OBJECTIVE

Human Resources – Employment / Staffing Assistant

SUMMARY

Efficient, high-energy, Human Resources Employment / Staffing Assistant with strong organization and administrative skills. Outgoing personality with excellent communications and interpersonal skills. Skilled in the use of resume and candidate tracking systems.

EXPERIENCE

DORCHESTER CORPORATION, Providence, RI   **2003 to Present**
Corporate headquarters of this 8,000-employee, $1.5 billion manufacturer of sporting goods equipment.

Staffing Assistant
Report to Manager of Corporate Staffing with responsibility for providing administrative support services to a staff of three professionals in the recruitment and hiring of over 300 new hires annually.

- Provides preliminary resume screening of over 30,000 resumes annually, referring resumes of qualified candidates to employment managers for final review.
- At the direction of employment managers, provides key word searches of electronic resume database for preliminary candidate identification – routing appropriate resumes for final review.
- Uses approved requisitions to list new job openings on company website.
- At the direction of employment managers, uses the Internet to place job listings on designated electronic job boards (e.g., Monster.com, Jobs.com, Hot Jobs, etc.).
- Coordinates candidate interview schedules, emailing published schedules along with resumes and evaluation forms to members of the interview team.
- Arranges and communicates candidate travel (transportation, meals, and lodging).
- Greets candidates upon arrival and arranges for same-day reimbursement of any out-of-pocket travel expenses.
- Escorts candidates to initial interviews, making appropriate introductions.
- Ensures receipt of interviewers' candidate evaluation forms prior to return of candidate for "close-out" at end of interview day.
- Coordinates management approval of terms of employment offers, advising employment managers of status.
- Orders and provides initial review of reference checks, referring identified issues to employment managers for resolution.
- Prepares and sends employment offer letters at the direction of employment managers.
- Coordinates arrangements for candidate pre-employment physical examinations.
- Uses Recruiting Solutions software to generate a variety of weekly and monthly staffing reports (e.g., interview-to-offer ratio report, offer-to-hire report, cost-per-hire report, employment requisition status report, etc.).

Sandra E. Bullock   **Page 2**

- Generates quarterly and annual candidate flow data report for use in E.E.O. affirmative action reporting.
- Answers and screens phone calls, types correspondence, and provides other miscellaneous administrative duties for the Manager of Corporate Staffing as required.

MANNINGTON CORPORATION, Springfield, MA Plant   **1999 - 2003**
Leading U.S. manufacturer vinyl flooring materials. The Birmingham plant employs 850 employees.

HR Administrative Assistant
Reported to Plant HR Manager, providing a full range of administrative support services to the plant's Human Resources function.

- Answered, screened, and directed incoming phone calls for HR Department staff.
- Screened, sorted, and distributed incoming mail to HR staff members.
- Composed and typed correspondence for Plant HR Manager.
- Scheduled appointments and maintained the Plant HR Manager's calendar.
- Prepared various PowerPoint presentations for use by Plant HR Manager in making presentations to employee groups and senior management.
- Prepared and typed a number of weekly, monthly, quarterly, and annual reports.
- Tracked department budget, advising Plant HR Manager of any negative variances.
- Performed others administrative duties as requested.

EDUCATION

High School Diploma
Providence High School, 1999

COMPUTER SKILLS

MS Office – Word, Excel, PowerPoint, Access Database
Recruiting Solutions – Resume & Applicant Tracking
Lawson - HRIS

MILDRED A. DIRKSON
903 Greentop Ridge
Chattanooga, TN 83495

Home: (814) 262-9837   Email: MilDrk@AOL.com   Office: (814) 263-3422

OBJECTIVE

Human Resources – Senior Administrative Assistant

SUMMARY

Highly personable, efficient Administrative Assistant with Human Resources background and excellent office and administrative skills. Well organized with the ability to effectively manage sizeable workload and juggle priorities as needed. Accustomed to handling highly sensitive, confidential issues and can effectively manage delicate situations calling for exceptional interpersonal skills. A careful listener with excellent verbal and written communication skills.

EXPERIENCE

JOHNSON CORPORATION, Chattanooga, TN   **1997 to Present**
A $3.6 billion, 15,000-employee, leading manufacturer of corrugated containers and fiber-based packaging materials.

Senior Administrative Assistant – Human Resources (2002 to Present)
Provide a full range of secretarial and administrative support services to the Human Resources Manager of this 1,200-employee corporate staff facility.

- Answers and screens all incoming phone calls, referring only those requiring the HR Manager's personal attention.
- Opens, screens, and sorts incoming mail, composing letters for HR Manager's signature in responding to routine inquiries.
- Screens and responds to routine emails on behalf of HR Manager, referring only those requiring personal answers or involving complex matters appropriately handled by the HR Manager.
- Greets employees and offers assistance regarding easily handled matters of routine nature.
- Types general correspondence, summaries, and reports.
- Schedules meetings and appointments for the HR Manager.
- Uses seasoned judgment, tact, and discretion in handling urgent matters of a sensitive or confidential nature, requiring the HR Manager's immediate attention.
- Manages department filing system, ensuring accuracy, organization, and ease of use.
- Oversees the distribution and administrative management of highly confidential employee programs such as performance reviews and salary administration.
- Prepares PowerPoint presentations and handouts to support large group meetings and senior management presentations.
- Drafts all personnel announcements and employee notices for posting on the company's electronic bulletin board.
- Provides other miscellaneous services as needed.

Administrative Assistant – Compensation & Benefits (1997 – 2002)
Reported to the Manger of Compensation, providing both secretarial and administrative services in support of the company's compensation programs.

- Answered, screened, and routed all department incoming calls.
- Opened, screened, sorted, and routed incoming mail to department members.
- Sorted, screened, and responded to routine email compensation inquiries.
- Maintained and safeguarded highly confidential employee compensation files.
- Maintained and updated the job description and Hay Group job evaluation files.
- Composed, prepared, and typed a wide range of correspondence and reports relating to compensation matters.
- Administratively managed the annual salary review program, including distribution, collection, and clerical review of all salary recommendation forms for the corporate staff (1,200 employees).
- Prepared PowerPoint presentations and handouts for use in employee group meetings and presentations to corporate management.

EDUCATION

High School Diploma
Chattanooga High School, 1997

COMPUTER SKILLS

MS Office – Word, Excel, PowerPoint, Access Database
SAP – HRIS
PageMaker 8.0
Crystal Reports

LYNN ANN BRODERICK

513 East Michigan Avenue
Apartment # 123-A
Chicago, IL 13246

Home: (512) 662-9413   Email: Lab513@AOL.com   Office: (512) 653-2997

OBJECTIVE

Administrative Assistant – Training & Development

SUMMARY

Conscientious, skilled Administrative Assistant with Major Corporation Training & Development background. Proficient, hardworking, service-oriented worker noted for ability to efficiently process huge work volume in a demanding, fast-paced work environment. Very strong interpersonal and communication skills coupled with a dedicated commitment to accuracy and high quality work standards.

EXPERIENCE

DEXTER COPORATION, Chicago, IL   **2002 to Present**
A $1.3 billion, 7,000-employee, leading manufacturer of filtration media.

Administrative Assistant – Training & Development (2002 to Present)
Provide a full range of secretarial and administrative support services to the Manager of Corporate Training & Development of this 7,000-employee corporation.

- Answers and screens all incoming phone calls for the Training & Development Department.
- Opens, screens, and sorts incoming mail, composing letters for HR Manager's signature in responding to routine inquiries.
- Prepares, publishes, electronically posts and emails quarterly schedule of training courses and seminars to managers and employee population.
- Handles and tracks all training program registrations, including management approvals and employee course completions.
- Schedules training rooms, including proper set-up and equipment availability.
- Coordinates and schedules internal and external (vendor) trainers for training programs.
- Distributes all advance materials, surveys, and required forms to all program participants.
- Arranges lodging and local transportation for out-of-town vendor trainers.
- Collects trainer evaluation forms from program participants and summarizes results for evaluation by members of the Corporate Training Staff.
- Schedules off-site training programs including training room reservations and set-up, trainer travel and lodging, and group room reservations to accommodate large group programs.
- Prepares PowerPoint presentations and a variety of other visual aids for use by training staff.
- Arranges volume printing of training manuals and other training handouts with internal print shop and outside printing sources.
- Types a variety of training-related general correspondence, summaries, and reports.
- Schedules meetings and appointments for the Manager of Corporate Training & Development.
- Manages department filing system, ensuring accuracy, organization, and ease of use.
- Provides other miscellaneous services as needed.

Lynn Ann Broderick **Page 2**

LEARNING SYSTEMS, INC., Chicago, IL **1998 – 2002**
A start-up company engaged in the custom development of e-learning programs for delivery over high-speed Internet connection.

Administrative Assistant
Reported to Company President with accountability for providing a broad range of secretarial and administrative support services.

- Answered and screened incoming phone calls.
- Opened, screened, and sorted incoming mail.
- Sorted, screened, and responded to routine email correspondence.
- Scheduled appointments and coordinated President's meetings and calendar using Microsoft Outlook.
- Made transportation and lodging arrangements in support of President's busy travel schedule.
- Composed and typed a wide range of correspondence and reports.
- Tracked expenses against approved budget, advising President of any negative trends or major variances from previously approved levels.
- Prepared PowerPoint presentations and handouts in support of President's presentations and sales & marketing efforts.
- Performed a variety of other administrative duties as requested.

EDUCATION

High School Diploma
Evanston High School, 1998

COMPUTER SKILLS

MS Word
Excel
PowerPoint
Access
QuickBooks Pro

CYNTHIA P. JONES
926 Clinton Avenue
Little Rock, AK 23928

Home: (525) 374-5590   Email: CynJon@AOL.com   Office: (525) 875-2213

OBJECTIVE

Executive Assistant / Senior Administrative Assistant – Human Resources

SUMMARY

Efficient, highly productive senior-level Administrative Assistance with over 15 years experience in the Human Resources Field. Friendly charismatic personality with excellent employee relations and interpersonal skills. Strong communicator, good listener, and excellent team player that enjoys working in a fast-paced, demanding, executive work environment.

EXPERIENCE

HASTINGS MANUFACTURING, INC., Little Rock, AK   **1991 to Present**
A $4.5 billion automotive parts manufacturer employing 23,000 employees worldwide (thirteen manufacturing plants and operations in sixteen foreign countries).

Executive Assistant – Human Resources (2001 to Present)
Report to the Senior Vice President of Human Resources with responsibility for providing a full range of secretarial and administrative support services in support of the corporate Human Resources function.

- Opens, screens, and responds to the Vice President's email and snail mail, referring only appropriate correspondence for direct response.
- Answers and screens all incoming phone calls, answering routine inquiries directly and routing unnecessary calls to appropriate HR staff members for response.
- Schedules meetings and appointments, maintaining an up-to-date calendar of events affecting the HR function.
- Coordinates and arranges all travel for senior HR staff members, including extensive international itineraries.
- Coordinates and expedites the preparation of a wide range of analyses and reports in support of HR strategic initiatives and programs, coordinating with HR department heads as needed.
- Assists in the preparation of important senior management and employee presentations to include the use of multimedia, PowerPoint slides, and printed support materials.
- Oversees the planning of major HR events, including facility reservations, menu planning, speakers, etc.
- Coordinates the compilation and organization of the Human Resources budget for annual budget review purposes.
- Monitors monthly budget performance, investigating reasons for budget variance and advising Vice President of reasons underlying significant variations.
- Daily interfaces with the Chairman, President, CEO, and all senior company officers, ensuring their questions are quickly and efficiently answered and that their HR needs are promptly met.

Senior Administrative Assistant – Human Resources (1997 – 2001)
Reported to Corporate Director of Human Resources with responsibility for providing a broad range of secretarial and administrative support services to the Director and his staff of 3 senior managers.

- Read, screened, and routed mail to all staff members.
- Responded to routine inquiries, referring only essential mail to the Director.
- Read and screened Director's email, responding to routine inquiries as appropriate.
- Answered, screened, and directed all incoming phone calls
- Maintained HR staff calendars through use of MS Outlook.
- Maintained all records and files for department.
- Coordinated and arranged meetings.
- Typed and prepared a wide range of correspondence including letters, memos, reports, PowerPoint presentations, and the like.
- Coordinated all travel itineraries including transportation, meals, lodging, special visas, etc. for both domestic and international trips.
- Performed analysis and prepared special summaries and reports as requested.

Administrative Assistant – Staffing   (1994 – 1997)
Administrative Assistant – Compensation & Benefits (1991 – 1994)

EDUCATION

High School Diploma
Clinton High School, 1991

COMPUTER SKILLS

MS Works
Word for Windows
MS Outlook
Excel
PowerPoint
Harvard Graphics
Access

KATHERINE A. CUNNINGHAM
625 Orchard Row
Morgantown, WV 18374

Home: (712) 345-5514   Email:KaCunn62@AOL.com   Office: (712) 345-9787

OBJECTIVE

Legal Assistant / Paralegal

SUMMARY

Skilled Legal Assistant / Paralegal with ten years experience in general law practices. Conscientious, thorough, hardworking, and accurate. Capable of efficiently handling large work volume under pressure and meeting tight deadlines. Strong interpersonal and communication skills.

EXPERIENCE

KRANE, SAUNDERS & WILKINSON, LLC, Morgantown, WV   **2004 to Present**
General practice law firm with some concentration in lemon law, consumer fraud, and residential real estate.

Paralegal
Provide paralegal and administrative support to the partners of a three-person law firm.

- Prepare all correspondence, pleadings, discovery, and motions in connection with legal cases involving lemon law, consumer fraud, auto accidents, criminal matters, municipal matters, and personal injury.
- Assist in all aspects of residential and commercial real estate transactions from sale contract through closing.
- Order and review title searches; prepare and review closing packages and closing documents.
- Perform administrative support duties to include assisting clients, typing, dictation, appointment setting, calendar maintenance, invoicing, billing, answering phones, etc.

COOPER, BARON & JACKSON, LLP, Baltimore, MD   **2000 – 2004**
General practice law firm with focus on matrimonial, auto accidents, personal injury, and general litigation.

Legal Secretary
Reported to Senior Partner with responsibility for providing a full range of administrative support services.

- Prepared correspondence, pleadings, and motions.
- Assisted in all aspects of real estate transactions from sale contract through final closing.
- Typed documents, arranged appointments, maintained calendars, answered and screened phone calls, maintained filing system, assisted clients, screened and distributed mail.

Katherine A. Cunningham   Page 2

WALTER REYNOLDS, ESQ., Baltimore, MD   **1996 – 2000**
Solo law practice with concentration in residential real estate law.

Real Estate Paralegal
Provided paralegal and administrative services in connection with real estate transactions.

- Prepared correspondence, closing documents, and settlement statements in preparation for residential real estate closings.
- Ordered and reviewed title searches.
- Prepared draft deeds and arranged for proper recording.
- Prepared routine sales agreements.
- Coordinated settlement details including funds disbursement.
- Set up escrow accounts and made bank deposits as required.
- Reviewed and notarized documents.
- Billed clients and maintained office filing system.

EDUCATION

Diploma – Paralegal Studies
American Business Academy, 1996

High School Diploma
Boyertown High School, 1994

SKILLS & ABILITIES

Computer Software: Windows 97, 98, 2000, and Me
                     MS Word, Works, WordPerfect
                     MS Outlook, Lotus 1-2-3, Lotus Organizer
                     CaseMaster, Easy Soft, Tabbs III
                     Hudworx, Allstate, Hot Docs

Office Skills: Type 65 wpm
                     Shorthand 55 wpm
                     Dictaphone
                     Notary Public of Maryland and West Virginia

Other: Speak fluent Spanish

ROBERT B. BRENTWOOD
6216 Ocean Meadows Road
Laguna Hills, CA 15248

Home: (949) 624-9837   Email:BoBre16@AOL.com   Office: (949) 552-9838

OBJECTIVE

Legal Assistant

SUMMARY

Skilled, industrious Legal Assistant with excellent training and experience in both general practice and criminal law. Efficient, thorough, accurate worker with excellent general office competencies complemented by strong communications and interpersonal skills. A solid producer who flourishes in fast-paced, demanding work environments.

EXPERIENCE

HAROLD KRATZMEIR, J.D., Newport Beach, CA   **2000 to Present**
Solo law practice with concentration in criminal defense.

Legal Assistant
Provided full administrative and legal support services to solo practitioner specializing in criminal law.

- Draft all court pleadings (Municipal and Superior Courts).
- Prepare and type client correspondence.
- Responsible for requesting discovery.
- Maintain and support heavy court calendar.
- Prepare extensive files for trials and collection proceedings.
- Provide training and direction to office staff as needed.
- Prepare, issue, and explain client invoices for legal services.
- Handle basic office accounting including accounts payable, accounts receivable, and payroll.

MILLER, DRAPER AND ROWE, LLP, Irving, CA   **1996 – 2000**
General law practice with concentration in workers' compensation, matrimonial, real estate, estate, bankruptcy and personal injury law.

Legal Secretary
Provided secretarial and administrative support services to law firm's Senior Partner.

- Prepared, typed, and filed a variety of legal documents and correspondence.
- Fielded and screened a heavy volume of incoming phone calls.
- Handled client questions, as appropriate, when attorney was unavailable or where direct contact with attorney was unnecessary.
- Maintained meticulous and up-to-date case and business files.

- Opened, screened and distributed mail.
- Scheduled depositions, conferences and appointments.

EDUCATION

A.A. Degree – Legal Studies
Newport Community College, 1996
Dean's List

High School Diploma
Newport Beach High School, 1994

COMPUTER SKILLS

MS Office – Word, PowerPoint, Excel
QuickBooks Pro Accounting Software

SANDRA L. LEVINE
4255 Cannel Street
San Antonio, TX 17729

Home: (814) 345-5514   Email: SanLe42@AOL.com   Office: (814) 447-8923

OBJECTIVE

Legal Secretary / Entry-Level Paralegal

SUMMARY

Skilled Legal Secretary / Entry-Level Paralegal with training and experience in bankruptcy, negligence, and general law. Efficient, highly productive worker who pays careful attention to detail and accuracy. Excellent secretarial and administrative skills combined with solid communication and interpersonal skills.

EXPERIENCE

WARLOW KLEINFELD, PC, San Antonio, TX   **2001 to Present**
Major business law firm with 16 offices throughout the United States.

Secretary II
Provide secretarial and administrative support services to law Partner in charge of business bankruptcy practice area.

- Prepares electronic bankruptcy filings.
- Drafts simple legal documents.
- Formats documents to conform to the appropriate court rules.
- Requests conflict checks.
- Opens new client cases and maintains complete, accurate, and up-to-date files.
- Performs full range of secretarial duties including typing letters, documents, and reports; answering and screening phone calls; reading, screening, and distributing mail; preparing invoices; scheduling appointments and meetings; maintaining calendars; organization and maintenance of filing system, etc.

SMITH & JOHNSON, LLP, Dallas, TX   **1998 – 2001**
Law partnership with specialization in bankruptcy filings.

Legal Secretary
Reported to Senior Partner with responsibility for providing a full range of administrative support services.

- Prepared electronic bankruptcy filings.
- Handled serving of objections.
- Requested conflict checks.
- Opened and maintained new client files.
- Provided full range of traditional secretarial support services.

Sandra L. Levine   **Page 2**

PEEBODY & TAYLOR, LLP, Birmingham, AL   **1996 – 1998**
Law partnership with primary focus on bankruptcy, real estate law, and commercial litigation.

Litigation Secretary
Provided administrative support to Senior Partners.

- Prepared filings for Superior, Chancery, and District courts.
- Prepared documents for real estate closings.
- Ordered and provided preliminary review of title searches.
- Prepared standard deeds following prescribed format as instructed.
- Prepared electronic bankruptcy filings.
- Provided full range of secretarial services.

EDUCATION

Paralegal Certificate
Birmingham Community College, 1996

High School Diploma
Birmingham High School, 1994

SKILLS & ABILITIES

Exceptional organizational and transcribing skills
Excellent computer skills
Type 75 – 80 wpm with high accuracy
Experience formatting pleadings and discovery documents

VICTORIA B. CARLSON, LPN
12 Sunset Valley Road
Sunnyvale, CA 23847

Home: (802) 556-9403   Email: ViCarRN@AOL.com   Cell: (892) 663-9985

OBJECTIVE

Staff Nurse – Skilled Care

SUMMARY

Sensitive, caring, and skilled nursing professional with 5 years experience providing patient care in a skilled care facility. Excellent team, interpersonal, and communication skills. Thorough, conscientious, and motivated to provide highest quality of professional services and personal care to resident patients.

EXPERIENCE

HOBART LIFECARE, INC., Sunnyvale, CA   **2003 to Present**
An 80-bed skilled-care facility providing a broad range of patient care services including illness care, restoration, rehabilitation, health counseling, and education.

Staff Nurse
Report to Director of Nursing with responsibility for providing full range of nursing and patient care services to elderly residents in a fast-paced, demanding, professional work environment.

- One of 5 staff-nursing professionals serving 80-personal skilled care resident population.
- Provide basic bedside care for sick, convalescing, and handicapped patients
- Prepare and administer medications in accordance with physician orders.
- Keep patients comfortable and provide emotional and psychological support.
- Take and record vital signs, administer injections, administer intravenous fluids.
- Apply dressings, apply ice packs and water bottles, give alcohol rubs and massages.
- Feed patients, recording solid food and liquid intake and output.
- Assist patients with bathing, dressing, and personal hygiene.
- Oversee nursing aids; assist in training new nursing professionals.

GREENTREE CONVALESCENT CENTER, Hillsdale, CA   **2000 to 2003**
A privately owned, 50-patient convalescent and skilled care facility catering to the elderly patient requiring life care services.

Charge Nurse
Report to Nursing Supervisor, providing third-shift healthcare services to a wing of 20 elderly patients requiring full range of skilled nursing services.

- Provided basic bedside care, including administration of medications, injections, and intravenous fluids under directions of Supervisor.

- Made periodic rounds, remaining attentive to the medical and emotional needs of patients.
- Took and recorded vital signs.
- Measured and recorded fluid intake and output.
- Assisted patients with personal hygiene.
- Applied dressings, ice packs, hot water bottles, where needed.
- Ensured the health, comfort, and overall well-being of patients.

EDUCATION

Diploma – Practical Nursing
Irving School of Nursing, 2000

High School Diploma
Newport High School, 1999

LICENSING & CERTIFICATIONS

LPN, State of California, 2001
License #; 23748597

MARY C. COOPER
106 Piney Ridge Drive
Ashville, NC 12317

Home: (802) 434-5792   Email: MarCoo@AOL.com   Work: (802) 436-9588

OBJECTIVE

Nursing Assistant

SUMMARY

Dedicated, hardworking Nursing Assistant with 6 years experience in community hospital environment providing nursing care in support of professional medical and nursing staff. Caring, attentive, and sensitive caregiver committed to the comfort and well being of patients.

EXPERIENCE

ASHVILLE MEMORIAL HOSPITAL, Ashville, NC   **2002 to Present**
A 350-bed community hospital providing health care services and related education to a community of 225,000 residents.

Nursing Assistant
Work under the direction of Nursing Supervisor or Staff Nurse providing support in attending to the medical, physical, and emotional need of hospital patients. Responsible for providing a wide range of services as follows.

- Provide for patient's personal hygiene; assisting with bathing, shaving, shampoos, etc.
- Provide bedpans and urinals, and give backrubs and massages.
- Assist patients with daily living activities such as dressing, eating, turning, and positioning.
- Observe and report unusual patient signs or symptoms to professional nursing staff.
- Administer enemas, ice packs, heat treatments, non-sterile dressings, etc.
- Answer patients' call lights, responding to their personal and emergency needs.
- Check and record vital signs, weight, fluid intake / output, and performs basic testing.
- Work effectively as a team member in delivering care to patients.
- Perform a variety of other tasks under the direction and supervision of professional nursing and medical staff.
- Provide for the overall comfort and personal needs of patients.

GREENVILLE GENERAL HOSPITAL, Greenville, SC   **1999 to 2002**
A 200-bed general community hospital serving the healthcare needs of the Greenville, SC area.

Nursing Assistant
Worked under the direct supervision of physicians and professional nursing staff, providing for the overall comfort and well being of patients.

Mary C. Cooper   **Page 2**

- Worked 2 years as a Nursing Assistant in Pediatric Unit.
- Worker 1 year as a Nurse's Aid in the Postoperative Care Unit.
- Provided for the daily living assistance needs of patients including dressing, bathing, ice packs, heat treatments, back massage, ambulatory assistance, etc.
- Provided emotional support, reassurance, and comfort as needed.
- Observed and reported unusual behavioral changes, physical complaints, and symptoms to professional nursing staff.
- Assisted professional staff in performing their general nursing duties.
- Provided wide range of duties in proving for the medical, physical, and comfort needs of patients.

EDUCATION

Certificate, Nursing Assistant Course
Greenville General Hospital, 1999

High School Diploma
Greenville High School, 1998

SANDRA E. BECKMAN, RN
25 Saltwater Cove
Ocean Pines, MD 23184

Home: (410) 552-6335   Email: SaBeck25@AOL.com   Office: (410) 552-8837

OBJECTIVE

Surgical Nurse – Cardiovascular Surgery

SUMMARY

Registered Nurse with 5 years cardiovascular surgical experience in a regional hospital ranked among the top 100 U.S. hospitals for its cardiology and cardiovascular surgical programs. Well trained, technically proficient, and skilled Surgical Nurse with commitment to provide the highest level of surgical nursing and post operative care to patients undergoing cardiovascular surgical procedures.

EXPERIENCE

SALISBURY REGIONAL HOSPITAL, Salisbury, MD   **2000 to Present**
400-bed regional hospital and healthcare facility serving the medical needs of tri-county area on Maryland's Eastern Shore.

Surgical Nurse – Cardiovascular Surgery
Report to Chief Surgeon with responsibility for providing full range of nursing duties in connection with cardiovascular surgical procedures.

- Assist physicians during surgery.
- Maintain and sterilize instrument packs and other supplies and equipment.
- Supervise preoperative room disinfection.
- Admit patients to operating room, checking all required records.
- Provide nursing services in operating room as scrub or circulating nurse.
- Set up surgical area, checking instruments and supplies.
- Assist anesthesiologist as needed.
- Position and re-supply sponges, instruments, etc. during surgery.
- Label and maintain records of specimens.
- Transfer patients to recovery room.
- Perform post-operative clean-up procedures.
- Inventory, order, and maintain stock of surgical supplies.

BERLIN HOSPITAL & MEDICAL CENTER, Berlin, MD   **1996 to 2000**
200-bed community hospital providing healthcare and emergency care services to Worcester County residents.

Sandra E. Beckman, RN   **Page 2**

Staff Nurse – General Surgery
Report to hospital's Chief Surgeon with responsibility for providing nursing services and assistance to physicians during general surgery.

- Assisted physicians during surgery.
- Provided preoperative disinfection services.
- Served as scrub or circulating nurse.
- Ensured readiness of operating room, and availability of needed instruments and supplies.
- Admitted patients to operating room, checking all required records.
- Performed post-operative clean-up.

EDUCATION

ADN, Salisbury State, 1996

High School Diploma
Berlin High School, 1994

LICENSING & CERTIFICATIONS

RN, State of Maryland, 2004
License # 235-6831

LYLE F. LANSING, RN
60 Waterloo Road
Buffalo, NY 13746

Home: (702) 556-9403   Email: LYLan60@AOL.com   Cell: (702) 556-9822

OBJECTIVE

Registered Nurse – Pediatric Care

SUMMARY

Registered Nurse with 8 years pediatric care experience in a community hospital environment. Sensitive, caring nursing professional with special ability to relate well to children and infants. Excellent interpersonal and communication skills with the ability to function effectively as part of a nursing team focused on providing best possible health care to pediatric patients.

EXPERIENCE

BUFFALO GENERAL HOSPITAL, Buffalo, NY   **1999 to Present**
500-bed community hospital providing health care education and services to an urban population of 350,000 residents.

Staff Nurse – Pediatrics
Report to Nursing Supervisor of 50-bed, Pediatric Unit, with responsible for providing for the overall healthcare and well being of pediatric patients.

- Plan, organize and oversee nursing functions to best support the medical, physical and psychological needs of pediatric patients.
- Initiate and implement individual patient care plans.
- Am attentive and responsive to patients' physical and emotional needs.
- Orients, trains and manages medical support personnel.
- Participate in the evaluation and development of support staff.
- Accurately and promptly carry out orders of Pediatric Unit Staff Physicians.
- Administer medications and intravenous solutions as required.
- Support and enforce infection-control policies and procedures.
- Ensure acceptable standards of patient care are met or exceeded.
- Maintain accurate and up-to-date patient charts and records.
- Participate in shift change meetings, ensuring complete communications and continuity of patient care.

SACRED HEART HOSPITAL, Buffalo, NY   **1996 to 1999**
150-bed Catholic hospital serving the medical needs of Southwestern Buffalo and proximate suburbs.

Lyle F. Lansing   **Page 2**

Staff Nurse – Pediatrics
Reported to Director of Nursing with responsibility for providing nursing care to a 15 patient Pediatric
Ward.

- Planned, organized, and directed nursing care plans to meet the medical and emotional needs
  of pediatric patients.
- Trained, assigned and directed the work of medical support personnel.
- Carried out the orders of Staff Physicians, administering medications, injections, intravenous
  solutions, etc.
- Made regular rounds observing and responding to patients' needs.
- Maintained accurate, up-to-date patient records and reports.

EDUCATION

ADN, Buffalo School of Nursing, 1996

High School Diploma
Buffalo High School, 1994

LICENSING & CERTIFICATIONS

RN, State of New York, 2004
License # 224-573-02

MARIE C. RATHERS
118 Claxton Street
Albany, NY 12830
Phone: (313) 554-9320
Email: MaRa118@AOL.com

OBJECTIVE

Painter / Drywall Installer

SUMMARY

Skilled painter and drywall installer with both residential and commercial construction experience. Efficient, hard-working craftsperson who pays attention to detail and takes pride in the quality of her work.

EXPERIENCE

WINSLOW INTERIOR DESIGNS, INC., Albany, NY   **2001 to Present**
Commercial and residential interior designer and painting contract firm.

Painter (2003 to Present)
Report to Construction Supervisor with responsibility for interior painting of private homes, apartment complexes, condominium complexes, and commercial retail properties. Painting contracts run the gamut from expensive, high-end custom homes to huge multi-unit condominium complexes.

- Measures jobs; estimating labor and material costs; prepares and submits estimates.
- Purchases and arranges for delivery of paint and related painting supplies.
- Prepares surfaces for painting.
- Fills cracks, holes and joints with caulk, putty, plaster or other appropriate filler using caulking gun or putty knife.
- Sands surfaces to smooth finish in preparation for paint application.
- Mixes and prepares paint for application.
- Paints surfaces with primer coat using spray equipment, rollers and paint brushes.
- Applies finish coat using appropriate application method.
- Sands surfaces prior to additional coats, as appropriate.
- Applies paint to simulate wood grain, marble, brick, or stonework.

Drywall Installer (2001 – 2003)
Reported to Construction Manager with responsibility for installing drywall in a wide variety of residential and commercial structures.

- Measured and estimated numerous jobs (both commercial and residential) for bid purposes.
- Ordered and arranged for delivery of drywall and related materials.
- Prepared surfaces for drywall application, countersinking nails and screws below surface level.
- Glued and nailed drywall to walls of structures.
- Applied joint sealing compound and tape to drywall joints.
- Lightly sanded surfaces in preparation for paint application.

EDUCATION

High School Diploma
Williamson Trade School, 2001

MARION T. ENGLISH
624 Boston Road
Springfield, MA 13295
Phone: (306) 925-4059
Email: MarEng@AOL.com

OBJECTIVE

Tile and Vinyl Floor Installer

SUMMARY

Skilled Tile and Vinyl Floor Installer with experience in the installation of a wide range of tile and vinyl flooring products in the foyers, kitchens, baths and recreation rooms of residential properties. Careful, conscientious and courteous worker who pays attention to detail and exhibits excellent interpersonal skills in dealing with residential customers.

EXPERIENCE

CRAEMER TILE AND FLOORING, INC., Springfield, MA   **1999 to Present**
Tile and vinyl flooring subcontractor providing subcontract services to residential builders and retail flooring outlets.

Tile Installer (2002 – Present)
Report to Installation Manager with responsibility for installing floor tile, ceramic tile, and slate in the foyers, kitchens, bathrooms, and recreation rooms of residential properties.

- Measures and estimates jobs, both materials and labor, for use in bid preparation.
- Plans project layout and specifies needed materials and supplies.
- Prepares surface for product installation, installing overlay on floors and/or washing concrete surfaces with washing soda and zinc sulfate solution.
- Sands floors, as needed, to ensure smooth surface prior to installation.
- Marks guidelines on surface for use in aligning product.
- Applies adhesive to floor or back of tile, pressing tile in place along guidelines and allowing appropriate spacing.
- Scribes and cuts tile to fit irregular spaces.
- Nails, screws, or glues wall molding to walls to add finishing touch.
- Cleans tile surface upon completion of job, removing scrap and debris.

Vinyl Floor Installer (1999 - 2002)
Reported to Installation Manager with responsibility for installing vinyl flooring in residential foyers, kitchens, bathrooms, and recreational areas.

- Measured and estimated numerous jobs for bid purposes.
- Specified and arranged for delivery of vinyl and related project supplies.
- Prepared surfaces for vinyl installation including overlay installation, sealing, and sanding
- Measured and marked floor with guidelines to ensure proper alignment of product.
- Applied adhesive to floor using trowel.
- Cut and fit product around appliances and other structural objects.
- Installed moldings and cleaned work site prior to departure.

ARCADIA BUILDERS, Rutledge, VT   **1997 – 1999**
Residential home and vacation house builder in Rutledge and surrounding areas.

Framing Carpenter
Reported to Construction Supervisor with responsibility for framing residential property including foundations, walls, floors, ceilings, and roof structures.

- Framed over 15 residential properties in a two-year period.
- Assisted builder in preparing bids, providing appropriate measurements and estimates of both lumber and labor costs.

EDUCATION

High School Diploma
Springfield Trade School, 1997

SKILLS

Use of a wide range of construction power and hand tools.
Proven ability to measure, estimate, and prepare accurate bids.
Tile installation, vinyl floor installation, and carpentry.

6

Cover Letters and
Their Importance

Whether you are responding to an employer's job advertisement in the newspaper, an Internet job board, or on the employer's own Web site, you are going to need a cover letter to accompany your resume when applying for a job. Likewise, if you decide to make a large mailing of your resume to a number of area employers, which can sometimes prove to be a very effective job-hunting technique, you will also need to include a cover letter along with your resume.

The cover letter you choose for sending your resume to an employer or perhaps an important networking contact can be one of the most significant factors in the success (or failure) of your job-search effort. A survey of nearly 600 Human Resource professionals and recruiters by the Society of Human Resource Management (SHRM), for example, suggests that some 76 percent of employers automatically eliminate an employment candidate based solely on the quality of his or her cover letter. The same survey suggests that some 43 percent of employers view the cover letter as being as important as the resume itself. (*Note:* A copy of the full survey can be obtained by contacting SHRM by phone, 703-548-3440, or by e-mail at SHRM.org.)

If your cover letter is well written and informative, it can grab the employer's attention, raise curiosity, and stimulate interest in your employment candidacy. If poorly written, it can be a disaster and cause the employer to quickly lose interest in you.

As an expert in the career and employment fields, I have always been surprised and amazed by the number of job seekers who will invest hours or days in preparing an absolutely outstanding resume, yet spend almost no time writing the cover letter which is the first thing that hits the recruiter's eyes. This is the job-hunting equivalent of wearing a neat, clean, starched shirt to the job interview, while wearing a crumpled, stained tie. The interviewer's attention is going to immediately focus on the tie, and the overall impression of the candidate is not going to be very good. This is the same effect that a poor cover letter can have. The employer may not even bother to look at your resume if the cover letter is a poor one.

The cover letter is the first thing that greets the recruiter's eye when removing your resume from its envelope. You've heard a lot about the importance of first impressions in the job interview and how this can affect the interview's outcome. The same thing is true of cover letters. It can have a major impact on how the employer perceives you right from the start.

Besides the letter's general appearance, *what* you say in the cover letter, and *how* you say it, can have a significant impact on the reader. How you express yourself in this important document can, for example, tell the employer a great deal about your communication skills. If well written, it may suggest to the employer that you are expressive, concise, and articulate—generally telegraphing you are an effective communicator. By contrast, a poorly written letter can suggest that your communications skills are badly lacking.

Additionally, the letter's organization and general physical appearance can also influence the employer's thinking. If the letter is poorly organized (doesn't have a logical flow), is sloppy in appearance (ragged margins, crowded text, coffee stains, etc.), it may suggest that this careless attitude may carry over to your work habits as well. Such an impression is not likely to be in your favor, and there is a high likelihood the employer will immediately move on to the next candidate.

The same is true of poor grammar, incorrect punctuation, and misspelled words. Many employers, in spotting these types of issues, are also likely to discard your candidacy and quickly move on to the resume of the next job seeker.

On the positive side, however, if well written and free of errors, the cover letter can *premarket* your candidacy. The positive feelings the employer gets from reading a well-prepared cover letter are likely to spill over to the resume as well as the job interview itself.

Although not applying to the majority of employers, from time to time I have heard some employers remark that they place more importance on the cover letter than they do on the resume. On more then one occasion, I have even heard it said that a decision was made to interview a job candidate based on the strength of the cover letter alone. Some employers have even gone further to state that in certain cases, had they received the resume alone (without benefit of the accompanying cover letter), they would not have agreed to interview the job seeker.

We can only conclude that having a well-written cover letter can be extremely important to the success of your resume submission, and the success (or failure) of your overall job-hunting campaign. Your cover letter, therefore, deserves deliberate and careful attention if you wish to ensure your job-hunting competitiveness and success.

Chapters 6 and 7 have been designed to provide you with careful, deliberate, step-by-step instructions for writing effective cover letters. As with Chapter 4, *Resume Writing: "By the Numbers,"* they provide easy-to-follow, step-by-step instructions for writing each section of the cover letter, one section at a time. Additionally, as with resume writing, a numbered sample is provided for both types of cover letters. By reading the description of each numbered cover letter section, and then actually seeing an example in the sample cover letter provided, you will readily understand what is needed.

In the following two chapters, we will be addressing two kinds of cover letters:

1. Advertising response letters and
2. Employer broadcast letters.

The advertising response letter, as the name suggests, is used when responding to an employer's job advertisement. This ad could appear in either a newspaper or on the Internet. An employer broadcast letter, on the other hand, is a general letter that is used to mass mail (or broadcast) your resume to a number of employers. It is used to mass market your resume in hopes of finding a job that has not yet been advertised by an employer. We will be discussing both of these kinds of letters in some detail in the following chapters.

7

Advertising Response Cover Letters

Recruitment advertising has long been an important source of jobs for those seeking employment. Although historically the term *recruitment advertising* has referred to classified advertising contained in the employment sections of the local newspaper, this is no longer the case. Today, job ads, even for hourly paid positions, are rapidly migrating to the online, Internet job boards, where employers can advertise for far less money than they paid for classified newspaper job ads. Although estimates vary, it is believed that recruitment advertising, both newspaper and Internet combined, accounts for somewhere between 10 percent to 14 percent of all jobs landed by job seekers. It is, therefore, an important source that you will want to use when searching for a position.

When responding to an ad, whether in the newspaper or on the Internet, you will need a cover letter to go along with your resume. If this letter is well designed and written, it can be a powerful ally in persuading an employer to bring you in for a job interview.

ADVANTAGES OF THE JOB AD

One key advantage of the job advertisement is that it tells you exactly what the employer is looking for in a desirable candidate. This can be a huge advantage when writing a cover letter in response to the ad. Too often, this fact is lost on the job seeker, however, and he or she misses a great opportunity to influence the employer's decision on who gets an invitation for a job interview and who does not.

As an experienced employment professional, I have often been amazed by the number of job applicants who respond to an advertisement for a job and have clearly elected to ignore the requirements of the position as spelled out in the ad itself. Instead, they go on and on in their cover letter, describing qualifications and skills that are in no way related to what the employer has said they are interested in. What a mistake this is.

Salespersons have long ago recognized the importance of understanding the needs of the buyer before they start their sales pitch. They then have the opportunity to adjust their sales presentation so that it is geared to the specific needs the buyer has said they are most interested in. Failure to do so, can result in a lengthy presentation of products and product attributes that are of little or no interest to the person who will be making the buying decision. The result, more often than not, is "no sale."

When it comes to responding to a job ad, there is much the job seeker can learn from top-flight sales professionals. You want to "give them what they want." Read the ad first to determine exactly what the employer is most interested in, and then use the cover letter to give them exactly what they are looking for.

THE BEN FRANKLIN BALANCE SHEET

If it was good enough for Ben Franklin, it's good enough for you!

Ben Franklin has long been credited as being the creator of the "Ben Franklin balance sheet," a technique that can be used to systematically analyze and compare different ideas or issues. This same technique can be used by you to systematically analyze a job advertisement in preparation for writing your advertising response cover letter. Here is how it works.

Start by taking a blank sheet of paper and drawing a vertical line down the center of the sheet. Label the left column with the heading "They Want." Now label the column to the right of your centerline with the heading "I Have."

Now, with the job ad immediately in front of you, thoroughly read the ad line by line. As you do, carefully list each of the employer's stated candidate requirements under the heading "They Want," using one line for each specific qualification mentioned in the ad. Be sure to list all qualifications stated in the ad.

Once you have listed all the employer's requirements on the left side of your paper, than carefully read the ad a second time, looking for clues about which of the employer's requirements, as stated in the ad, seem to be more important than the others. Usually the most important qualifications will be listed first, but this is not necessarily the case.

In reading the ad, look for key words or phrases that are clues that the employer feels that certain of these qualifications are more important than others.

Some key words to look for include the following:

- Must have.
- Highly desirable.
- Important.
- Required.

Use of these words provides strong clues about which of the candidate qualifications the employer is most interested in—which the employer views as being most desirable.

Next, number each of the candidate qualifications you have entered on your list in the order of their importance. Start with the number 1, as being the most important qualification, 2 the next most important, 3 the next most important, and so on, until you have numbered or ranked all qualifications contained in your list.

Once all qualifications have been ranked in order of their importance, then prepare a second balance sheet, relisting the qualifications in the order of their ranking in the left-hand column under the heading "They Want." You now have a prioritized listing of the employer's candidate requirements, in the order of their importance to the employer.

Now, using your newly prepared resume as the basis, prepare a corresponding list of those qualifications that you possess that closely match the employer's requirements. You will want to record these next to their corresponding counterparts, but in the column headed "I Have."

Once you have completed the Ben Franklin balance sheet, you are in a great position to write a very effective cover letter that is specifically tailored to the needs of the employer. You now need to incorporate this information into the cover letter, one that is likely to have very positive impact on the employer and persuade the company's recruiter to invite you for a job interview.

LETTER COMPONENTS

Using the sample cover letter on the next page, you will note that the cover letter has five basic components, each of which has been numbered for easy reference. These components are:

1. Ad reference.
2. Statement of interest.
3. Qualification comparison.
4. Response request.
5. Appreciation statement.

I will now systematically walk you through each of these letter components, one at a time, so you will have a chance to fully understand and see what goes into each of these elements. By following this process, you will be able to use each component and its corresponding description as the basis for modeling your own letters. This should simplify the letter-writing process considerably and make it quite easy for you to construct a very effective cover letter. Let's start with the "Ad Reference."

1 2 Ad Reference and Statement of Interest

Employers can sometimes run hundreds of employment advertisements at a time. So simply stating that you are "responding to their ad" is not going to mean very much. They need to know exactly which ad you are responding to, so they can compare your qualifications with those contained in that specific advertisement. Without this information, they are left to wonder in which job you are interested. If they can't figure this out relatively quickly, they are likely to pass on

600 Pine Street
Albany, NY 18374

April 22, 2005

Mr. John F. Frankfurt
Employment Manager
Ransom Manufacturing Company, Inc.
200 River Road
Albany, NY 18347

Dear Mr. Frankfurt:

1 & 2   I am very interested in the position of Administrative Assistant, which was advertised by your company in the April 21st edition of the *Albany Register*. I am therefore enclosing my resume for your consideration.

3   Review of your requirements, as stated in this advertisement, suggests that I would be an excellent candidate for this position. Please consider my relevant qualifications as follow:

- High School Diploma, Albany High School, 1996
- 9 Years Experience as an Administrative Assistant in the Procurement Function
- Heavy Experience in Typing Purchase Orders, PO Releases and Contracts
- Corporate Office Experience in a Manufacturing Company Environment
- Strong Word Processing & Computer Skills
- Skilled in the Use of MS Word, Excel, PowerPoint, and Harvard Graphics
- Good Organization and Filing Skills
- Able to Handle Large Work Volume in Fast-Paced, Demanding Environment
- Excellent Team Player with Strong Interpersonal and Communication Skills

4   Should you agree that I am a good fit for this position, I would welcome the chance to further explore this opportunity during a personal interview. I can be confidentially reached during the day at my office (phone: 617-775-0928), or via email at LinDahl@AOL.com. Please also feel free to call me at my home during evening hours.

5   Thank you for your consideration, and I look forward to hearing from you shortly.

Sincerely,

Linda A. Dahler

Linda A. Dahler

Enclosure

your resume and move right on to the next candidate. Obviously, you do not want this to happen.

In writing the first paragraph of your cover letter, you will want to accomplish two things. First, you will want to state that you are interested in their job opening. Second, you will want to refer to the specific ad to which you are responding. This is accomplished by stating the name of the publication in which the ad appeared, the date on which it appeared, and the title of the position advertised. Here are a couple of examples:

Example 1
I noticed your advertisement in the March 2nd edition of *The Philadelphia Inquirer* for a Forklift Truck Operator and am very interested in applying for this position.

Example 2
Your advertisement for a Shipping Clerk in the April 20th issue of *The Daily Globe* is of great interest to me, and I am, therefore, enclosing my resume for your review and consideration.

You will also note in these opening statements, that the job seeker expresses strong interest in the position. Simply telling the employer that you are sending in your resume in response to their ad isn't going to do it. As in these examples, you need to enthusiastically state that you are interested in the job they have to offer. Showing genuine interest in the position can help set you apart from other candidates applying for the same position. Employers like to feel they are hiring someone who has a strong interest in the position they are filling and are therefore likely to be with them for the long haul. So, be sure to state your interest in the position.

③ Qualifications Comparison

Remember the Ben Franklin Balance Sheet you just completed a little while ago? Well, here is where you will use it.

The second paragraph of the cover letter begins a very positive statement to the effect that you would appear to be an excellent match for the company's requirements. This is then followed by the list of your related qualifications as listed in the "I Have" column of the Ben Franklin Balance Sheet analysis you completed for that job. Here are two examples of how this is to be accomplished.

Example 1
A review of your requirements for this position, as stated in your advertisement, suggests that I would be an excellent match for this position. My qualifications include:
• Certified forklift truck operator.
• Five years shipping and receiving experience.
• Wireless computer inventory systems experience.

- Worked in automated warehousing environment.
- Solid skills in basic math.
- Team player with good communications skills.

Example 2

Based on your ad and my qualifications, I would appear to be an ideal candidate for this position. My qualifications include:

- First class, licensed electrician (state of Pennsylvania).
- Two years apprenticeship program—Williamson Trade School.
- Seven years maintenance experience in industrial manufacturing.
- Strong power and power distribution background.
- Heavy experience with manufacturing control systems.
- Familiarity with Honeywell TDC 3000 and Related Instruments.

As you can see in each of these examples, the job seeker has stated that he or she appears to be well qualified for the position advertised by the employer, and then goes on to list those specific qualifications the employer cited in their advertisement, highlighting each using a bullet point.

This is an excellent way for you to respond to the job ad, since it makes it easy for the employer to see that you possess the very qualifications they listed in their advertisement. It provides an easy checklist for the employer and encourages the reader of the cover letter to read the attached resume and/or proceed to call you for the purpose of setting up a job interview. Listing your qualifications using this linear (line-by-line) approach makes it simple for the employer to quickly see that you have the qualifications they want, without the need to try to find these qualifications in the resume that accompanies your cover letter.

A word of caution, however: If you do not have all of the qualifications sought by the employer, or if you are missing some of the key qualifications being sought, you *do not* want to make use of this type of "linear" approach. In such cases, providing the employer with this automatic checklist could work to your disadvantage. It would make it too easy to see that you are missing some of the requirements they feel are important to filling the job.

If you have done your homework by preparing a Ben Franklin balance sheet analysis of the employer's ad, it should be readily apparent that you are missing some of the basic qualifications being sought by the employer. In this case, instead of using the linear approach as illustrated above, you are going to want to present your qualifications for the position using a "literary" approach. By this I mean, simply presenting your qualifications in paragraph form.

Here are some examples of this literary approach that you can use to model your own qualifications comparison.

Example 1

My background suggests that I should be an excellent candidate for this position. Please consider my following qualifications. I am a graduate of

Pfeiffer Trade School, where I completed a 2-year program in mechanical drafting. I have over 5 years experience in the design and drafting of paper machine head boxes and wire sections. In addition, I have considerable experience using CAD and have excellent written and verbal communication skills.

Example 2
Review of your requirements suggests that I am well qualified for the position you advertised. My background includes 2 years working as a Chemical Technician in the Quality Control Laboratory of a manufacturer of polyurethane foam. I am skilled in the use of a wide range of test instruments and testing protocols, and am well versed in design of experiments and statistical techniques. I have also undergone extensive total quality training at the Deming Institute, and am noted for having excellent written communication and interpersonal skills.

As you can see from the above examples of the literary approach, using this literary format makes it more difficult for the employer to spot any missing qualifications. Had you instead chosen to use the linear approach, illustrated earlier, these "qualification voids" would have been much easier to spot, making it far too easy for the employer to eliminate you from further employment consideration.

The lesson to be learned here is quite simple. If you have most or all of the employer's requirements (especially the critical ones), use the linear approach to highlight this fact. On the other hand, if you are missing key qualifications, don't make this too easy for the employer to see. In this case, use the literary or paragraph approach.

4 Response Request

The next section of the cover letter, as illustrated in paragraph #4 of the sample cover letter, states that you are interested in interviewing for the job and provides basic contact information, making it easy for the employer to contact you. Here are some examples of how to accomplish this:

Example 1
Should you agree that my qualifications are a good match for your requirements, I would welcome the opportunity to interview for this position. Although difficult to be reached during the day, I can be reached via e-mail at (CarVat@AOL.com) or at my home phone (605-997-4356) during the evening.

Example 2
I am very interested in the position of Shipping and Receiving Clerk and would pleased to further discuss my background and experience with you during a personal interview. Please feel free to contact me by e-mail (DooRap@MSN.com). I can also be reached by cell phone (463-339-9485) during the day, if necessary.

5 Appreciation Statement

Good manners can go a long way toward creating a favorable impression. So, don't forget to express your appreciation for the employer taking the time to read your cover letter and resume and for the consideration given to your employment candidacy.

Here are two brief examples:

Example 1
Thank you for your consideration. I look forward to hearing from you.

Example 2
I appreciate your consideration and look forward to hearing from you. Thank you.

Some additional sample advertising cover letters follow. Study them and use them to your advantage in writing your own cover letters.

SHIFT MECHANIC

Fortune 100 cereal and food manufacturer seeks skilled Shift Mechanic to work in its Baltimore Plant packaging operation. Successful candidate will report to the Shift Supervisor with responsibility for the maintenance, troubleshooting and repair of high-speed packaging equipment.

Position requires mechanical maintenance training and at least 4 years experience in the installation, troubleshooting and repair of high-speed packaging machinery. Successful candidates will be skilled in the precision setting of high-speed timing mechanisms requiring close tolerances.

We seek an individual with training in total quality and statistical process control with strong knowledge of preventive & predictive maintenance. Must be a solid team player with excellent communications & interpersonal skills.

Qualified candidates, please email or send resume to:

Rhonda T. Wilson
Employment Manager

Tilton Manufacturing Co.
216 Fall River Road
Baltimore, MD 18236

(Email: EM@Tilton.com)

Equal Opportunity Employer

421 Berkley Road
Silver Springs, MD 18274

November 12, 2004

Ms. Rhonda T. Wilson
Employment Manager
Tilton Manufacturing Company
216 Fall River Road
Baltimore, MD 18236

Dear Ms. Wilson:

I was excited to see your ad for a Shift Mechanic in this Sunday's edition of _The Baltimore Sun_. This seems like an excellent job opportunity, and I feel I have the background and experience you are looking for.

Here is a brief summary of my qualification highlights, which appear to be an excellent match for the requirements cited in your advertisement.

- Diploma, Wharton Trade School, Mechanical Trades (2 –year program)
- 6 Years Shift Mechanic at Bennington Manufacturing Company
- Experience in Installation, Troubleshooting and Repair of High-Speed Packaging Equipment
- Skilled in Setting Timing Mechanisms Requiring Precision Setting and Close Tolerances
- Trained in Total Quality and Statistical Process Control
- Extensive Training in Predictive and Preventive Maintenance
- Solid Team Player Who Enjoys Working with Others in a Team Environment
- Excellent Communications and Interpersonal Skills

I would welcome the opportunity to meet with you to share more of my background and further explore this interesting opportunity. Should you have an interest in interviewing me, I can be reached via email or at my home phone during evening hours. Both are listed on the enclosed resume.

I appreciate your consideration of my candidacy, and look forward to hearing from you. Thank you.

Sincerely,

Michael R. Johnson

Michael R. Johnson

Enclosure

Packaging Machine Operator

Leading manufacturer of sanitary tissue products seeks experienced Packaging Machine Operator to work second shift at its Darien, Connecticut Plant. You will report to the Second Shift Supervisor, and work as part of a high-performance work system team responsible for the converting, finishing and packaging of our high-quality Baby Soft facial tissue product.

Competitive hourly pay rate and outstanding benefits package are provided.

We seek an experienced Packaging Machine Operator who holds a high school diploma or equivalent and has worked in paper converting and finishing operations. Requires strong mechanical aptitude with skills in the use of basic hand tools.

The successful candidate will have worked in a high-performance, team-based environment and possess a solid work ethic and excellent interpersonal skills.

Qualified candidates, please email or send resume to:

**Barbara D. Fullerton
Recruiter**

The Baxter Corporation

1600 Industrial Road
Darien, CT 13589

(Email: Recruiter@Baxter.com)

Equal Opportunity Employer

824 Lorenzo Drive
Darien, CT 13749

October 2, 2004

Ms. Barbara D. Fullerton
Corporate Recruiter
The Baxter Corporation
1600 Industrial Road
Darien, CT 13589

Dear Ms. Fullerton:

The advertisement that you ran on November 31st in the *Darien Local News* for a Packaging Machine Operator is of great interest to me. I am therefore enclosing my resume in application for this position, and hope you will give my qualifications serious consideration.

My review of your ad suggests that I am an ideal candidate for this position, and that my skills and abilities match your stated qualifications almost perfectly. Please consider my following qualifications:

- High School Diploma, Darien High School, 1995
- 5 Years as Packaging Machine Operator – Wilson Company
- 2 Years Slitter Operator – Strumford Paper Company
- 2 Years Shift Mechanical Adjuster – Strumford Paper Company
- Skilled in the Use of Wide Range of Hand Tools
- Worked in a High Performance, Team-Based Environment
- Solid Work Ethic and Excellent Interpersonal Skills

I have been a valued contributor to our Packaging Team and am credited with several recommendations that led to greater department productivity and efficiency.

I think you would be pleased with my qualifications, and would very much appreciate the opportunity to interview for this position. I can be reached by email or at my home phone, both of which are provided on the attached resume.

Thank you for considering my credentials, and I look forward to hearing from you in the near future.

Sincerely,

Grace P. Schockley

Grace P. Schockley

Enclosure

Quality Control Technician

Leading manufacturer of intermediate chemicals seeks skilled QC Technician for Quality Control Laboratory at its Sandusky manufacturing facility. Position reports to QC Manager with responsibility for performing wide range of lab tests to ensure quality of its chemical product line.

Successful candidate will hold an Associates Degree in chemistry from an accredited college and have a minimum of 4 years QC Technician experience in the chemical process industry. Must be well trained in instrumental techniques, including GC, and be familiar with a wide range of lab instruments and testing methods.

Should be skilled in design of experiments, statistical process control, and Total Quality Management (TQM). Must be thorough, methodical, and efficient worker with good written and oral communication skills.

Qualified candidates, please email or send resume to:

Craig T. Peters
Quality Laboratory Supervisor

The Fuller Company, Inc.
822 Bay Street
Sandusky, OH 12359

(Email: CTPeters@Baxter.com)

Equal Opportunity Employer

225 West Grove Street
Huron, OH 13968

June 15, 2005

Mr. Craig T. Peters
Quality Laboratory Supervisor
The Fuller Company, Inc.
822 Bay Street
Sandusky, OH 12359

Dear Mr. Peters:

Your ad for a Quality Control Technician, as advertised in the _Cleveland Plain Dealer_ on June 14th, caught my eye! Although not actively seeking a new position at this time, this position sounded particularly appealing and has prompted me to submit my resume for your review and consideration.

A comparison of your requirements with my qualifications suggests this could be an excellent match. Please consider the following:

- Associates Degree, Chemistry, University of Toledo, 1994
- 6 Years Quality Control Technician – Toledo Chemical Corporation
- Trained in Instrumental Techniques including Gas Chromatography
- Familiarity with Wide Range of Lab Instruments and Testing Methodology
- Trained in Design of Experiments, Statistical Process Control, and TQM
- Thorough, Methodical, Accurate, and Efficient Worker
- Good Written and Oral Communication Skills

If you agree with my assessment of job fit, I would welcome a call from you to arrange for an employment interview. I can be reached by email (BruSam@AOL.com) or by cell phone (614-228-3092).

I appreciate your consideration for this job opening, and will look forward to hearing from you. Thank you.

Sincerely,

Bruce D. Sampson

Bruce D. Sampson

Enclosure

Mechanical Draftsperson

Engineering design services company seeks skilled Mechanical Draftsperson with strong CAD experience. Position reports to Senior Design Engineer with responsibility for providing design and drafting support in the design of high-speed web-handling equipment.

Position requires formal mechanical drafting training and 2 to 4 years experience in the design drafting of paper finishing and converting equipment or equivalent web-handling equipment.

Desire strong CAD skills with exposure to instrumentation and control system machine interface. Must be comfortable working in a fast-paced, high-pressure environment with tight project deadlines.

Interested candidates, please email or send resume to:

Keith W. Langsford
Manager of Human Resources

Wheeler Engineering Services
215 Green Ridge Road
Boulder, CO 21846

(Email: KWL@Wheeler.com)

Equal Opportunity Employer

306 Wellington Avenue
Denver, CO 21847

March 22, 2004

Mr. Keith W. Langsford
Manager of Human Resources
Wheeler Engineering Services, Inc.
215 Green Ridge Road
Boulder, CO 21846

Dear Mr. Langsford

I was pleased to see your ad in the _Boulder News_ on March 20th for a Mechanical Draftsperson with strong CAD background. This position appears to be an excellent match for both my career interests and background, and I am therefore enclosing a resume for your consideration.

Careful review of this advertisement, and the credentials you are seeking, seems to suggest I am well qualified for this position. Specifically, my qualifications include:

- Diploma, Mechanical Design, Boulder Technical Institute, 2000
- 4 Years Draftsperson – Pierson Design, Inc.
- Machine Design & Drafting of High-Speed Web-Handling Equipment
- Experience in Design of Paper Finishing & Converting Machinery
- Heavy CAD Experience
- Exposure to Instrumentation & Control System Interfaces
- Work Effectively in Fast-Paced, High Demand Environment with Tight Deadlines

Assuming you agree I have the qualifications and experience you are seeking, I would welcome the opportunity to further explore this position during a personal interview. Please feel free to contact me by either email (WalJon@MSN.com) or cell phone (204-762-9938) at your convenience.

I appreciate your consideration for this position, and look forward to hearing from you in the near future.

Thank you.

Sincerely,

Walter P. Johnson

Walter P. Johnson

Enclosure

8

Employer Broadcast Letters

As mentioned briefly in Chapter 6, the employer broadcast letter may be used to either mass mail your resume to a number of employers, or to send your resume via e-mail to employers who you have reason to believe might have an interest in hiring someone with your qualifications. Although statistically this approach is generally less productive than other employment sources such as networking, advertising, and employment agencies, resume mass mailing does have a definite place in the job search process.

Over the years, my firm, Brandywine Consulting, has extensively used the mass mailing approach to help people find employment. The general positive response rate from this type of mailing typically ranges between 3 percent to 6 percent. In a tight labor market, where jobs are few and job seekers are many, the result will be closer to 3 percent. In the opposite kind of market where there are many job openings but few qualified candidates, results of a broadcast mailing of your resume is likely to be closer to 6 percent or even better.

In a tight labor market, should you decide to mail your resume to 100 employers, you will likely have three employers contacting you with interest in your background. Of the three, our experience has been that one of those three companies, after a brief phone interview, will decide they are not interested in going further. One company you are likely to screen out due to your lack of interest in the position they have to offer, leaving only one position in which there is mutual interest. In summary, in a 100-piece mailing, the probabilities are there will be only one position that has high potential for a good match.

In a more liberal job market, where jobs are plentiful and competition is less intense, the odds of a large resume broadcast mailing working are about double, with about 6 percent of employers typically responding with interest to your resume. Thus, a 100-piece mailing will yield about six positive responses. Our experience shows two of these employers, after a brief telephone interview, will decide to not to proceed to the onsite interview, and in another two cases you will decide you are not interested in the type of position they are offering. Thus, in the improved job market, a 100-piece mailing will probably net you only two mutually interesting job openings.

Sounds like a lot of work for only a small result, doesn't it? Well, it is, but if it is the right job for you, it may well be worth all the effort.

Where Brandywine has made these kinds of mailings, we have typically mailed the applicant's resume to a much larger group of companies (usually 500 to 600). This would then yield between five to twelve (depending on labor market conditions) interesting job opportunities. Surfacing this many realistic job opportunities in a short time (typically two to three weeks) is an impressive result. So large broadcast mailings can have excellent payoff, if you are willing to invest the time, energy, and expense of getting one together.

TIME SAVINGS

One thing that suggests that a broadcast mailing, using standard postal mailing, may be worth the investment is the time savings. Think about it for a moment. In a matter of a week or so, you can have a large 500- or 600-piece mailing out there working for you.

How long would it take you to contact each of these companies by phone, and at what cost? It would take months. Worse yet, what if you tried visiting this huge number of companies for purposes of picking up a job application. This could take years.

So, in a matter of a week or so, with some research effort on your part and a fairly modest expenditure, your mailing can reach several hundred employers. And, while this mailing is out there working for you, you can begin to use other employment sources, such as newspapers, Internet job boards, and networking to simultaneously conduct your job search. Following this approach is bound to cut down job search time and produce better results much faster than if you tried to contact each of these employers personally.

REACHING THE HIDDEN JOB MARKET

One advantage of using the broadcast mailing approach is that it provides you with the opportunity to reach what is frequently called the "hidden job market." These are the new jobs that are just surfacing and which employers have not yet had opportunity to advertise.

At this point, you may think that your broadcast cover letter should be sent to the human resources or employment manager. Forget this idea! You do not want to send your resume to this department. Instead, you want to send it directly to the department head who would most likely be hiring you. Thus, if you are a Forklift Truck Operator, you will want to send your resume to the Manufacturing Manager or Operations Manager. If you are an Accounting Clerk, you will want to send it to the Accounting Manager. If you are a Janitor, address your letter to the Facilities Manager, and so on.

The functional manager (the Manufacturing Manager, Accounting Manager, Facilities Manager, etc.) to whom you will be sending your cover letter may not yet have notified the human resources department that they have a job opening to fill. If your cover letter hits just at the time they are thinking about filling a new job, and you have the right qualifications, you could be going in for a job interview the very next day. Had you sent your broadcast letter to the human resources department, they would not have known the job was open and would have exhibited no interest in your employment candidacy.

Although it is preferable to address your broadcast cover letter to your target manager by name, it may be very difficult to get this information. If not possible or too difficult to get these names, simply address your letter to the appropriate job title without using a specific name. In all likelihood, your letter will be opened and read by the functional department you have targeted, and if there is a suitable opening they will get back to you. If not, they will simply forward your letter and resume on to the human resources department for appropriate response and filing.

Another advantage of the broadcast mailing is that it can not only be a quick way of surfacing job opportunities, but it can also substantially reduce your competition. This is particularly true if the job is new and has not yet been advertised by the employer. Think about the logic of this! Once the job has been advertised, thousands of people are aware of it and may be applying. On the other hand, if the job is unadvertised and still "hidden," there would be no competition. Would you rather compete with thousands or with zero others for the job? Obviously, you would rather be the only applicant for the position.

GENERATING A MAILING LIST

If you want to generate a mailing list and also keep the cost down, you may want to try your state employment service. Many have huge computer databases of local employers and can help you quickly create a large target mailing list for your broadcast mail campaign.

Another possibility is your local or county library. Many times these libraries also have access to large databases of area companies and, with the help of the librarian, you will be able to generate a list of target companies.

One other source to consider is your county Chamber of Commerce. For an investment of $25 or $50, you can probably acquire their membership directory, which can sometimes contain hundreds, if not thousands, of area employers. Additionally, you might contact the local Small Business Association to see what resources they may have available to add to your list. They can probably point you in the right direction.

AUTOMATED RESUME DISTRIBUTION

With the advent of Internet recruiting and the rapid expansion of job hunting on the Internet, there are now a number of firms springing up that, for a fee, will automatically e-mail your resume and cover letter to hundreds or even thousands of employers. This can be a huge timesaver and can get your resume out there quickly.

Although fees for such Internet resume broadcast services can vary, an expenditure of about $100 or so is likely to get your cover letter and resume sent to several thousand employers practically overnight. Many allow you to target specific geographical areas, such as a given city and its suburbs, while others e-mail your resume to a huge database of national companies only. You will need to research this. To find such companies, use your Internet search engine to find the words "resume distribution," "automated resume distribution," "resume e-mailing services," and similar descriptive categories.

One such Internet site, Resume Rocket, for example, at the time of this writing claims they will send your resume via e-mail to some 15,000 companies and another 8,000 employment agencies for a fairly modest fee in the $100+ range. Imagine the time and expense involved if you were to attempt to prepare a huge e-mail mailing of this magnitude on your own. It would take months and cost a small fortune.

It should be pointed out that this concept of automated Internet resume broadcasting is somewhat new, however, and is yet to be proven. I have not seen any research to date that shows how effective this method is. If these firms do what they say they do, instantly forwarding your resume via e-mail to thousands of employment contacts, I would have to think the law of averages is greatly in your favor. Perhaps by the time I write the next edition of this book, research will be available that allows us to gauge the effectiveness of this technique. In the meantime, you may want to think about giving it a shot.

As suggested earlier in this book, if you do not own a computer or don't know how to use one, it is time to seek the help of a relative, neighbor, or friend. Locating these types of Internet resume distribution companies is fairly simple and can be done in perhaps 15 minutes or less. They can also help to get you signed up for the service and electronically send your resume to these firms. You will want to have a credit card handy when you do, as they will want to be paid for their services.

THE EMPLOYER BROADCAST LETTER

Whether you will be using an Internet service company to e-mail your resume to a large number of employers, or plan to use the slower "snail mail" (the U.S. Postal Service), you will need to prepare a cover letter to go along with the resume. This type of letter is called a "broadcast cover letter," since you will be "broadcasting" your resume to a large number of employers. The balance of this chapter will help you prepare such a letter.

As in the last chapter, I will be walking you through each step of the cover letter, one paragraph at a time. To help make this process easy, I have included a sample cover letter, with numbered sections on page 179. Before we get started, you may want to take a few moments to study this sample broadcast letter.

1 Introductory Paragraph

The first paragraph of the employer broadcast cover letter is known as the introduction or introductory paragraph. Although there is no one single way to write this paragraph, it is intended to accomplish two or more of the following objectives:

- Catch the reader's attention.
- Convey the type of position you are seeking.
- Provide a broad, thumbnail summary of your qualifications.

In addition to the numbered sample letter, there are four additional examples of broadcast cover letters provided at the end of this chapter. Each introductory paragraph, although designed to accomplish two or more of these objectives, is different from the other. These were intentionally written this way so that you would have the opportunity to see several approaches typically used by job seekers when writing this initial paragraph.

You will notice that some of these letters begin by asking the employer a question. This is a technique often used to engage the reader and capture his or her interest.

It is suggested you read each of these sample letters and choose the paragraph that you like most and that best suits your individual needs. Then use this sample paragraph as the basis for tailoring your own introductory paragraph that will grab the employer's interest and encourage them to read your resume.

2   Qualification Highlights

Section number 2 of the sample resume is a good example of a paragraph designed to highlight your key knowledge, skills, and competencies. Important qualifications, those that employers are likely to find most attractive, should be highlighted using bullets so they stand out and command the reader's attention.

Here again, the intent is to grab the reader's attention, providing just enough important qualification highlights to generate interest and compel the employer to read the resume you have enclosed for that very purpose. When selecting and ordering these qualifications, chose those that are most readily recognized as important or critical to successful performance of the type of work you are seeking.

When selecting qualifications to be highlighted, start first by listing technical competencies—things like relevant education, specific knowledge, and critical skills essential to a high level of job performance. Then list some of the personal traits and characteristics important to performing the job as well as those important to working and communicating with others. Many employers are looking for the social skills that are important to getting along with others and functioning as an effective member of the team. You will want to make a point of highlighting some of these as well.

When selecting these positive personal attributes for inclusion in this section of the cover letter, you may find it helpful to revisit the list of *Positive Personal Descriptors* contained in Chapter 4 (page 40). This will help suggest personal traits and characteristics that are important to include, but you may not have thought of them. The list will help stimulate your thinking.

1526 Prairie Highway
Austin, TX 12395

September 22, 2005

Ms. Lisa W. Krantz
Production Manager
Texstar Paper Company, Inc.
32 Canal Street
Austin, TX 12386

Dear Ms. Krantz:

1 I am a knowledgeable, skilled Production Mechanic with over 12 years experience in paper converting and finishing operations. I am considered a talented troubleshooter with solid mechanical skills and the ability to diagnose, adjust and rapidly repair line equipment while "on the run".

2 I am in the process of making a career change, and have enclosed my resume for your review and consideration. Key highlights of my qualifications include:

- Diploma, Mechanics, Austin Trade School, 1993
- 2 Years – Second Shift Mechanic – Tissue Finishing – Porter Paper, Inc.
- Provide Mechanical Troubleshooting & Repair to 4 Finishing Lines
- 8 Years - Mechanical Adjuster – Towel Converting/Finishing – Dexter Paper Co.
- Expert training in the fine-tuning of sensitive electromechanical equipment requiring close tolerances and split-second timing adjustments.
- Skilled In Troubleshooting and Repair of Instrumentation & Control Systems
- Experienced in Machine Audit & Preventive Maintenance Programs

In addition to my technical skills, I am an excellent team player with good interpersonal and communications skills. I enjoy working in a team-based environment.

3 If you are in the market for a seasoned Production Mechanic with Paper Industry background, one who can "hit the ground running", I would be pleased to have the opportunity to interview with your company. My contact information is provided on the accompanying resume.

4 I appreciate your consideration, and look forward to hearing from you. Thank you.

Sincerely,

Michael S. Walters

Michael S. Walters

Enclosure

Review of the sample cover letters at the end of this chapter should also provide you with some good ideas on the kinds of qualifications you will want to include in this qualifications highlights section.

③ Request for Interview

As shown in section ③ of the sample resume, this paragraph either requests or suggests that an interview take place. Job seekers also typically use this section to provide contact information, making it easy for the employer to reach them.

This section of the resume is pretty straightforward and, by reviewing the sample resumes at the end of this chapter, you will easily get the hang of it. Use these examples to craft your own request for interview section.

④ Appreciation Statement

The final paragraph of the employer broadcast cover letter, as you can see from the resume samples, is also very straightforward. It is designed to express appreciation for the employer taking the time to read your cover letter and review your resume. A simple thank you is a nice touch and suggests that you have some basic social graces.

16 Kenilworth Lane
Atlanta, GA 23184

August 16, 2003

Manager of Quality
Biscayne Polymer Corporation
22 Palmetto Drive
Biscayne, FL 23117

Dear Sir / Madam:

Could you use a skilled Lab Technician – Quality Control, with extensive background in the Polymer Industry? If so, I think you will find my background interesting!

I am a skilled Senior Quality Control Technician with more than 8 years quality control laboratory experience with a manufacturer of polyurethane intermediates, including TDI and resins. Some qualification highlights include the following:

- 5 Years – Senior QC Lab Technician – Piper Polymer Specialties
- 3 Years – QC Lab Technician – Piper Polymer Specialties
- Skilled in the use of wide range of instruments and testing equipment including AA, LPS, FTIR, GC and HPLC.
- Experience in carrying out a wide spectrum of QC tests and protocols
- Exposed to executing IQ/OQ protocols and reports for new equipment
- Skilled at performing method and instrument verifications
- Experienced in training of new lab techs in testing procedures & protocols

I am a "fast study", who likes to keep current on new QC instruments and testing methodologies. I have brought many creative ideas and new approaches that have saved my employer both testing time and money. I am highly motivated to always look for new and more efficient ways to carry out QC testing and improve overall laboratory operations.

I have enclosed a resume for your review and consideration, and would welcome the opportunity to explore career opportunities with your company.

If my background and qualifications are of interest, please contact me by email (BWA16 @MSN. com) or at my home during evening hours (610-364-9937).

Thank you for your time and consideration. I look forward to hearing from you.

Sincerely,

Gwendolyn W. Peters

Gwendolyn W. Peters

Enclosure

205 Wilson Avenue
Cincinnati, OH 23857

February 21, 2004

Production Manager
Textron Company, Inc.
500 East River Road
Cincinnati, OH 23866

Dear Sir / Madam:

As the Production Manager of a textile manufacturing plant, I am sure you are always on the lookout for talented, motivated employees who will work hard and make a solid contribution to your manufacturing operations. I am such a worker!

Should you, or one of your Shift Supervisors, currently have an opening in your operations for a skilled production worker, I would ask that you give serious consideration to my qualifications, which include the following:

- Certified Forklift Truck Operator
- 5 Years - Packaging Machine Operator - Wilson Manufacturing
- 2 Years - Warehouse Worker – Dexter Corporation
- Skilled in Use of Wide Range of Hand Tools
- Trained in Statistical Process Control & TQM
- Experience Working in Team-Based Manufacturing Environment

I have excellent interpersonal and communications skills, and am noted for being an efficient, productive worker. References will tell you that I am a motivated, dedicated, and hard-working employee that will always give my employer 110%!

I have enclosed my resume for your review and consideration.

Perhaps I could meet with you or one of your production staff to further explore the contributions I can make to your operations. I can be reached via email or by telephone during the evening. Both email address and phone number are provided on the enclosed resume.

Thank you for your consideration, and I look forward to hearing from you.

Sincerely,

William R. Davidson

William R. Davidson

Enclosure

308 North Darlington Street
West Chester, PA 19382

July 27, 2005

Warehousing & Distribution Manager
The Phillips Corporation
913 Industrial Parkway
Essington, PA 19236

Dear Sir / Madam:

Do you have room in your warehousing and distribution services team for an energetic, hard-working Receiving Clerk or Warehouse Worker who enjoys working in a busy, high-volume work environment? If so, I would welcome your call!

I am a skilled Warehouse Worker / Receiving Clerk noted for accuracy and efficiency in overseeing the receipt, transport and storage of equipment, raw materials, and vital supplies in a fast-paced, demanding manufacturing environment. Highlights of my qualifications include:

- 3 Years – Receiving Clerk – Flegal Manufacturing, Inc.
- 4 Years – Truck Driver – Warfield Security Company, Inc.
- Certified Forklift Operator
- Skilled in Use of Technology in a Modern, Automated Warehousing Operation
- Experience in Use of Wireless Computer Inventory Technology
- Skilled in Use of Hand Tools
- Solid Team Player with Good Interpersonal Skills
- Highly Accurate, Efficient, and Dependable Worker

I enjoy an excellent reputation as a high-energy, dedicated and productive worker who is committed to the success of my company. I know you would find me to be a valuable and positive contributor to your warehousing and distribution team!

If you currently have a suitable job opening in your operation, I would welcome the opportunity to meet with you personally. My contact information has been provided on the enclosed resume.

I appreciate your consideration, and look forward to hearing from you. Thank you.

Sincerely,

David B. Williamson

David B. Williamson

Enclosure

1621 Tyson Road
Gary, IN 23164

May 16, 2003

Mr. Gerald R. Mason
Corporate Controller
Millington Corporation
322 Industrial Highway
Gary, IN 23228

Dear Mr. Mason:

A skilled, highly organized, motivated Administrative Assistant, I have provided excellent administrative support services to a number of senior level executives. My outstanding performance and commitment to high quality work have earned me several accolades as well as promotions throughout my career.

I have recently decided to make a career move, and am submitting my resume for your review and consideration. My background and experience as an Administrative Assistant in the controller's function may be of particular interest to you. The following briefly highlights my relevant qualifications:

- Diploma, Administrative Services, The Martin School, 1989
- 5 Years – Executive Administrative Assistant to Corporate Controller
- 4 Years – Senior Administrative Assistant – Accounting & HR
- 2 Years – Administrative Assistant – Corporate Accounting
- 2 Years – Senior Accounts Payable Clerk
- 1 Year – Accounts Payable Clerk
- Type 85 WPM with High Level of Accuracy
- Software Proficiency: SAP, MS Word, Excel, PowerPoint, Harvard Graphics

I am noted as a highly efficient, productive worker, but also possess strong interpersonal and communication skills as well. I enjoy working in a fast-paced, demanding environment, and have an excellent track record in meeting tight deadlines.

If my background is of interest, I would welcome the opportunity to meet with you personally for the purpose of exploring opportunities in your organization. My contact information is provided on the enclosed resume.

Thank you very much for your consideration, and I look forward to hearing from you.

Sincerely

Susan B. Clark

Susan B. Clark

Enclosure

Index